WINNERS' HABITS

3 Steps to Powerful Success Routines

Exercise More, Live Healthier, Work More Productively, and Have Better Relationships

by

Patrick Drechsler

Table of Contents

Introduction

The neighbor again!

He must have gotten up at 5 a.m. for his morning exercise as usual. There's no other way to explain why his music resounds so penetratingly through the walls and reaches you in bed. You pull the covers over your head and just want to sleep on. After your day finally begins at 10 a.m., you meet him outside while taking out the trash and he's bursting with *joie de vivre*. He proudly tells you that he's spending his Sunday working on a dream project, and that he will soon be able to quit his day job and make a living from his hobby instead. He even believes he is on his way to financial freedom.

Is he crazy? Or is he just attracting success with his positive habits, getting closer to a dream that seems almost inconceivable to you because your own, self-destructive habits are getting the better of you? You feel like you are stuck on the hamster wheel in a job you don't like with monotonous free time, because you are not very open to new hobbies and interests.

Why is it that some people create a happy and cohesive family life and do great things together, while others barely talk to each other and watch TV?

I too was trapped on my personal hamster wheel for a long time before I figured out which principles lead to success. I had a well-paid job as a lecturer, but it offered few opportunities for career advancement. The topics I presented were always the same. I didn't really know what to do with my days off as I lacked a positive outlook. I got into the habit of doing things that didn't help the situation. I slept late, and before I knew it the day was half over. During breaks from lectures, I always ate the bad canteen food. When I didn't feel like that anymore, I switched to snacking, and even quit sports. *If I eat an unhealthy diet, I won't be able to do any sport anyway...* I thought to myself, as one negative thing led to another. Eventually, reading numerous books, plus some other experiences, helped me form more positive habits. Sports came back into my life, while healthy eating, and getting up early became easier. Thanks to learning how to cultivate positive habits, I got involved in an environmental protection association, in addition to my career. Even though my futureless job remained at first, life around it changed for the better. In the end, even my profession was positive, as I focused on the good aspects of it, and developed more pleasure in my work.

It is not for nothing that the statement, "we humans are creatures of habit" has been a German proverb for decades. What humans do, they do to a large extent, out of habit. But what is a habit anyway?

A habit can be described as "acquired behaviors that are difficult to resist." But habits aren't just about behavioral patterns, they are acquired ways of thinking too. Because before the action always comes the thought pattern. A person can acquire as many habits that promote success as he wants if he could only just be aware of this.

To this end, a large part of this guide is devoted to the question of how to reprogram your thinking and align it with your goals. Several practical exercises are included that will help you acquire a positive attitude towards life. Scientific evidence, and many interesting theories, will show you how important and powerful, a positive attitude is.

After learning to retrain your thoughts, the book will focus on retraining your habits through exercises laid out in the later chapters. There is plenty of support and guidance to help you find your own unique path to success. After all, every person has his own view of what success actually is.

The exercises will show you how to build useful habits through reward setting, which can be practiced repeatedly until your life starts to transform. When these useful habits are combined with the elimination of negative habits, you get closer to your goal of becoming successful.

A lot of people believe that the way to change your life habits is to consciously resist a bad habit until it is gone, but this can actually be quite challenging because it's so easy to give in as soon as a small negative event occurs in your life, unless you have worked at it with the proper strategies as described in this book.

Here is a list of some of the questions you might be thinking about right now:

> How do I manage to establish a basic positive attitude?
> Which habits help me to achieve this?
> How do I ensure sustainability in my habit changes?
> How do I find out what success means to me personally?

- ➢ What are my priorities?
- ➢ What do I need to motivate myself at the beginning, during, and after the transition to a new me?
- ➢ Do I need to be disciplined?
- ➢ How do I determine which actions will lead me to success?
- ➢ What methods do I use to fight negative habits and establish positive ones?
- ➢ Can special products help?
- ➢ Which habits are particularly well-known and recommended?
- ➢ Which micro habits are universally transferable?

This book will answer all of these questions and put you in an informed position, so that you will be able to choose your path forward to having successful habits that transform your life.

What does success mean to you?

Opinions differ on the definition of success. Some take the easy way out and talk about achievement in the sense of increased assets, fit bodies, and other external factors that can be measured by the opinions of other people, or the standards of society. While others understand that internal success is defined solely by their own criteria.

Those who have inner success as a goal tend prioritize their own desires and choose activities that correspond to their own real interests. While those who aspire towards external success will be guided by the ideas of other people. Keep in mind that you interact with many different people in your life, each with his own idea of what success is. So, you can never succeed in satisfying everyone around you and perpetual external success becomes unrealistic in the long run.

If you prioritize your own interests, desires, and goals, the probability of succeeding is higher because you will have more motivation. Undoubtedly, there will be decisions, here and there in life, where you will also have to follow the interests of other people, like making decisions at the board level of a company, planning a vacation with your partner, and so on. So, we will also focus on that later in the book, but for now the focus is completely on you. Define inner success for yourself!

My wishes, my goals, my interests – my success!

If you want to find out which goals reflect inner success for you, you have to pay attention to your feelings. Feelings, just like habits, come from within and are shaped by our past experiences. Feelings can actually *be* a form of habit. For example, if you are used to being a "couch potato" every night, watching TV on the sofa, and consuming pizza and Coca-Cola, this will make you feel good and safe for now. It can be a way of rewarding a hard day at work. But the feelings in that moment are not everything.

Start listening to your thoughts and feelings when you are away from those moments. It is not uncommon for overweight people to feel good whilst consuming unhealthy foods, because they are giving in to an urge, and getting gratification from it. But this satisfaction is only temporary, as are the feelings. In the many other situations during the course of a day, negative feelings are not uncommon among overweight people because:

➤ Mocking looks in public cause discomfort.
➤ Possible health issues cause anxiety and insecurity.
➤ More barriers to the realization of one's own goals, e.g., cannot wear desired wardrobe or pursue desired activity.
➤ Looking in the mirror causes dissatisfaction.
➤ Lack of mobility as time passes.

The situation is similar in other areas:

➤ Partnership: When you are spending time with your partner, and you watch TV together in the evening as a form of relaxation. But you end up spending every evening together in the same way, because it has become a habit. If you go purely by the moment, you feel happy. But, if you think about it more deeply, you realize that this monotonous evening routine is actually making you unhappy, because you aren't fulfilling your deeper desires. It's time to make a change, but you only realize the need for change when you question yourself on a deeper level.

➤ Occupation: You have been working in your chosen profession for twelve years now; things are automated, and undemanding. Every day you perform your duty and go about your daily routine. At heart you are a varied, articulate, and adventurous person. Generally, you are happy all round, although your job is more of a necessary means to finance your life than anything else. When you take a close look at your feelings, you realize how dissatisfied you really are with your job, and that all you need is a new career for a perfect life. You will come to this realization if you regularly sit down in peace and reflect on the feelings that your job gives you throughout the day.

➤ Education / Study: Your entire family works in the industry in which you are now to train / study. Your family takes your career path for granted, so you choose it according to them despite having many other talents. As a result, your performance leaves a lot to be desired. But because you regularly reflect, you realize early on that the path you have chosen is not the right one for you, which is why your performance is lacking. You then change to another training program or another course of study.

There are many secrets lying dormant in us human beings. And while secrets from other people can have a protective effect, the secrets we keep from ourselves lead to unhappiness, because we run the risk of making decisions that are not in accordance with our real desires. Consequently, our actions will be marked by lower motivation.

Am I really a career person or more of a family person?

Do I want to achieve success only in terms of sports and health because I am already satisfied in all other areas of life?

Is it important for me to include external success, at least in part, because I owe a lot to my parents and want to make them proud?

You should think carefully about the answers to these questions. How to understand your own thoughts and emotions correctly and make the right decisions, will be explained often throughout the book. It is important that you are attentive and open to it. Because lasting inner happiness and success is only possible if you reflect and find for yourself what your heart and mind truly desire.

Find suitable habits for your own success

Every positive habit has its benefits. Some habits can even promote success in multiple ways. At this point we will make a distinction between macro, and micro habits. Macro habits are relatively general, like healthy eating. Micro habits are more specific, like eating fruit twice every night.

If you want to acquire habits that bring success, the best way is usually through micro habits. You select several micro habits that combine into one big macro habit. This macro habit is usually synonymous with your goal or at least a big part of it.

Finding suitable habits for your own success, means nothing other than considering which habits contribute to achieving your goal. The goal is defined beforehand, through comprehensive consideration. To achieve the goal, both types of habits are important, with the small ones coming mostly at the beginning. If you were to use only macro habits to make the changes however, you would find the process more difficult, because you could fall back into old behavioral patterns.

Here, are three examples of useful micro habits, that ensure that this doesn't happen:

1. Your goal is to use your day more effectively and avoid wasting so much time.
    Useful micro habits: Getting up earlier, making small to-do lists, and writing diaries. Bigger habits would be getting up very early (several hours earlier than usual) or keeping a detailed schedule for the day.
2. You set yourself the goal of reducing stress in everyday life and taking more time for yourself.
    Useful micro habits: Set up break times in your daily routine that you strictly adhere to and switch off digital media and chat programs in the evening. Macro habits include meditating regularly every day and doing a regular "digital detox" for several days or hours each week.
3. You feel you are too ungrateful in your life for the privileges you enjoy compared to others from less affluent regions of the world.

Useful micro habits: Start keeping a list of what you are grateful for at the end of each day. The extension of this micro habit are macro habits such as building an environment of positive people around you, and meeting with them regularly. Their positive and grateful attitude toward life can influence you in a purposeful way.

Note: This guidebook wants to support you on your individual path. Accordingly, there will be no rigid guidelines on what you have to do to succeed. Rather, you can expect a customizable collection of ideas and methods. Among them are habits that have great potential to promote success. One of these habits is to keep your thoughts and feelings optimistic. You will learn how to do this, and why it is important, in the third chapter. But first, we will focus on the findings and theories about the properties of habits, in order to understand why negative habits tend to be so ingrained, despite the fact that positive habits lead you to success more easily.

The nature of habits

How do habits develop?

Even though the research on habits has few really robust theses, at least several similarly insightful, smaller approaches exist.

All of the types of habits presented in this guidebook recognize certain triggers as their cause. These triggers reflect our attitude towards life and are the motivation to perform certain actions. Triggers that start with our own negative emotions (e.g., doubts, fears, laziness etc.) lead to the development, and consolidation of negative habits. These habits carry over to other areas of life, so they partially shape our character. As an old Chinese proverb says, "Watch your thoughts, for they become words. Watch your words, for they become actions. Watch your actions, for they become habits. Watch your habits, for they become your character. Watch your character, for it becomes your destiny."

Negative habits highlight certain basic negative attitudes that should be changed in order to get closer to personal success. The more of these negative triggers are present, the more strongly habits become anchored, until at some point they become automated. These automations are success killers. While positive habits on the other hand, make success much more likely.

Four processes that establish habits

In his work *The 1% Method* (2020), James Clear, who is now considered an expert on habits, describes the processes that foster them. He identifies triggers, cravings, routines, and rewards as the driving forces of habits, precisely in that order. While the first process made a habit arise, the further processes would gradually contribute to its consolidation, according to the author.

The processes can apply to both positive and negative habits as we will highlight by comparing the habit of going out partying every weekend and being regularly involved in an association.

Trigger

Attending a party, and consuming alcohol brings people together on the one hand, and lifts barriers on the other. The mood becomes more relaxed, the sense of shame decreases, and everyone is on the same level.

Registering in a non-profit association gets you involved with other people, while contributing to a cause that is close to your heart. The common interest also removes barriers to socializing.

Request

The second process in Clear's model, occurs when a thing appears desirable. This happens precisely when value is added by the trigger. A person who takes it a little too easy at their first party and embarrasses themselves to the bone (possibly even ending up in the hospital with alcohol poisoning and having to meekly explain themselves to mom and dad), will not develop a great desire for parties, at least for a while. The risk of getting used to parties every weekend and maintaining one's circle of friends only when drunk, decreases. On the other hand, the feeling of increased self-confidence and exuberance, due to drinking at parties, can lead to drinking regularly or in larger amounts. A "consolidated circle of friends" can develop in this environment which pre-programs a negative habit.

In contrast, a positive habit can develop in the case of charitable activities in an association, if the mood is good and the club's objectives are achieved. Such activities are often perceived positively by the public, which creates additional value and can strengthen the desire to make a habit out of it.

Routine

Routine ensures that the respective habit can be practiced more easily so the process becomes automated. In the context of our examples: Through acquired friends at parties, networking increases and on the way to the party there are agreements in the group on a different driver who does not drink alcohol. The same applies to associations, where carpooling is used on excursions or out-of-town commitments, private appointments etc.

Reward

Reward, the 4th and final process, provides even more incentive to repeat a habit. In the case of parties, being known as gregarious, or even the king of the party, can be perceived as a reward. In the association, rewards depend on the particular field of activity. For example, if you are in a group for nature lovers, and you have participated in the creation of new green areas in the city, you will have a visual reward every time you pass the area. In a sports club, the trophies and medals would be satisfying evidence of your success. Perhaps, in addition, you will meet a person with whom you develop a special friendship, and you will benefit from a social contact and more support in your life.

What you can take away from Clear's model

Clear's model breaks our habits down into processes to help us understand the nature of the habit, identify how strong it is engrained in us and how it got there. It also shows us how to replace negative habits with more positive ones. After all, if you can make something attractive and reward yourself for it, you can also make something else unattractive and punish yourself for it.

Lewin model of change

Kurt Lewin's model of change explains how to develop new behavioral patterns through the displacement of old ones:

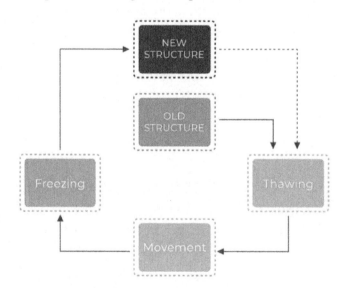

Figure 1: Lewin model of change

Starting point difficult to overcome

Old structures that prevail in a person serve as the basis and starting point of this model. You may consider the old structures as your current habits which you wish to replace by new structures or better habits.

According to Lewin, the individuals concerned are often aware that a behavior needs to be changed. However, he said, emotions are an obstacle, because of the deep-seated predisposition to habit. Since everyday processes would need to change, insecurities would arise. These are unwarranted, according to Lewin, because the goal is never to make complete changes. Instead, the goal is to change part of one's habits step by step, in order to adapt to the environment, expand one's own behavioral repertoire and, in the long term, master the complete change of habits.

1st phase: thawing

If one equates negative habits with a block of ice, in order to enable a change in behavior, thawing would be the appropriate means. Thawing is the process of gaining the motivation to change the behavior. You may assume that you are already, at least partially, in this phase, because if you hadn't identified a problem, you probably wouldn't be reading this guidebook.

Thawing encourages people to confront their negative habits. The process is set in motion by recognizing that their previous habits are not purposeful. Failures, dissatisfaction, loneliness and similar negative states or regularly recurring events, and serve as the motivation for a change of behavior, once highlighted.

Phase 2: Movement

As soon as something is in motion, something is happening; actions lead to change. Lewin's approach is about trial and error, until the best approach can be found for each person.

Phase 3: Freezing

Lewin's model describes freezing as a phase of change. Should a change increasingly become habitual, it would be frozen and become a new structure. Freezing he says, requires a change that has been successfully accomplished. It is tantamount to the acquisition of a new habit. Lewin argues, that looking back at the old structures and making clear the added values of the new structures, promotes the sustainability of the change. This leads to a stabilization of the new state.

What you can take away from Lewin's model

Lewin's model primarily addresses the process of habituation, which is a useful extension to Clear's model that highlights the formation of habits. Parallels between the 2 models exist in that habits are considered deeply embedded in the person in both cases. Lewin refers incidentally to the role of emotions in change, whereas Clear goes into particular depth here, providing an explanation of how the emotional significance of habit occurs. A change in the affected person's view of the old, or existing structures, is necessary in both models, to establish new and more beneficial structures. Although the 2 authors did not work together, both models complement each other extremely well.

In the following chapters of this book, the insights from Lewin's model will help you to make the transition process more effective. By means of practical exercises, you will be given sustainable concepts for making the transition successful over the long term. If everything works out, you won't just be riding the wave of success for a short time, but as often, and for as long, as you want.

Habit loop: Scientifically based

Very briefly, we will now discuss the habit loop model, as it is largely similar to that of Clear. What differentiates the habit loop is that it triggers rewards and cravings that are increasingly related to each other:

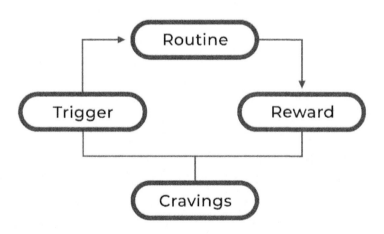

Figure 2: Habit loop model

In contrast to Clear, who sees craving as a second process in the habit loop, craving as a trigger, and longing for the reward, are given more emphasis. This underscores the powerful impact of human emotions in the context of habits; after all, craving, as a combination of the words "crave" and "addiction," is a deeply rooted emotion. To feel longing is to be addicted to something. So, the habit loop emphasizes the intensity of craving, which is why Chapter 3 places a high priority on controlling your emotions. Appropriate exercises will help you to become master of your emotions and to use this purposefully for changes of habit.

How much time does it take to get used to the new system?

You may have heard, through your own research on the Internet, in books, or in conversations, that changes of habit generally take 21 days. A negative habit would have to be replaced by a positive one, and this positive habit would have to be practiced for 21 days in order to get used to it. Where this time estimate comes from and what it is based on is not known. One possible origin could be the best-selling book *Psycho-Cybernetics* (1960) by Dr. Maxwell Maltz. The author, a plastic surgeon, performed cosmetic surgery on patients who still disliked their appearance immediately afterwards. About 21 days after surgery, however, they were happier with their appearance, he said. The doctor attributed this to the patients getting used to a certain self-image they had of themselves. They had been used to being dissatisfied with their visual appearance. In addition to this "habit" (Dr. Maxwell Maltz never uses the word "habit" in his book; note), he observed how patients suffered from phantom limb pain for up to 21 days after amputations too.

The reasoning is that Dr. Maltz's practical experiences may have been picked up by habit theorists and applied to habit research. This seems plausible. It could be that after 21 days, for certain types of habits, a change of habit is successfully accomplished but there is no guarantee of this. Instead, it would be better to assume that a change of habit will take more time.

The extent of the habit, the type of habit, and your individual character, all affect how quickly you change from a negative to a positive behavioral pattern.

> **Extent of habit**: Habits that you have already cultivated for several years, or decades are more difficult to displace than fresh habits. Especially habits that brought you positive things in earlier times have a nostalgic or emotionally high value that is difficult to dislodge.

> **Type of habit**: A habit may be closely linked to worldview. Such habits of cultural, religious, or experiential value are persistent. They require a partial adjustment of one's character. In contrast, there are habits that are hardly linked to beliefs, but which you already know are disadvantageous. Here, readjustment is easier.

> **Your character**: You will have a very unique attitude, especially toward the practical tasks that begin in the second chapter of this book. One person will think the exercises are silly, while another will get down to business with fervor. This much can be said: The person who is the most willing at the beginning, and who cooperates the most, will make the fastest progress.

At best, you're looking at an adjustment period of several months. A recent British study conducted by Lally, Cornelia et al. (2009), which included 96 participants, and was about getting used to morning exercise and healthy food and drink, found: that the subjects needed between 18 and 254 days, until they had reached a stable level of habituation. Only then could there be talk of a new habit. The mean value for the habit was a duration of 66 days. Since then, some other sources have also reported 66 days as an average timespan for the formation of new habits.

Step 1: Conversion begins in the mind

Our actions lead to success. If you look at all the movers and shakers who are attracting attention these days, you won't be able to avoid the conclusion that their reputation is due to actions.

Elon Musk is admired by some people, not because he talks about revolutionary business ideas, but because he puts them into practice against all odds. In China, they are partially changing the laws for Musk, and in the USA, the Corona regulations for his factories were relaxed. When things get tight for one of his companies, he is the first to work night shifts at the factory and treat his stress-related sleep problems with pills. None of this is sustainable or healthy, but it *is* success at first glance.

Greta Thunberg's success can be traced back to her habit of sitting in front of the Parliament building every Friday. Her persistence, and unwillingness to compromise even in front of the world's greatest politicians and personalities, paved the way for the visible results her movement for environmental protection is achieving.

Even if you look further back and take a closer look at the origin of Germany, you will see in Charlemagne a man who entered the history books through his actions. He proselytized the Saxons and expanded his Frankish empire. Driven by the mission to expand Christianity, his career took him to the gates of Rome, where he had himself crowned emperor, as a German king. This was the beginning of the Holy Roman Empire, which only came to an end after almost 1,000 years at the hands of Napoleon Bonaparte.

You can think what you want about these people. However, they were or are, undoubtedly successful in their own way. Actions led them to success. But human actions are preceded by something: thoughts. These are accompanied by another large and difficult to control component, namely feelings. Successful actions do not come out of nowhere. They come from a combination of thoughts and feelings.

In order to establish habits in the long term and in a goal-oriented manner, you should work your way through, step by step to the actions. This approach requires that you first deal with the upstream system, the thoughts and feelings. This system must be trimmed to success by habit, so that you can also make the actions successful with full conviction.

This is also illustrated by the three personal examples given above: Elon Musk became aware of inequalities during his childhood at the time of apartheid – he was born in South Africa – whereupon he made it his goal to want to change the world. His deeply held beliefs led to thoughts and feelings that made him stick to his goals and take action. Greta Thunberg's unwillingness to compromise and persistence are due in part to her illness, which has a considerable influence on her thoughts, and makes it almost impossible for her to weigh up differentiated arguments. Greta Thunberg will probably always pursue her goals with everything that makes her tick. Charlemagne, on the other hand, according to historical lore, met the Pope in early childhood. His vow to proselytize the pagans into Christians and to spread the Christian faith, as well as his irrepressible faith in God, led him to have the fixed conviction that he had to extend Christianity by all means in his power. And so it came to pass.

Feelings and thoughts come at the beginning. To retrain them and make them successful is the key to a simplified practice. Exercises exist for retraining thoughts, but the brain is too complex to be reprogrammed as desired by a few simple exercises alone. Therefore, let's first take a look at how the brain works.

Feeling, thinking, sensing, acting

In his work *Fühlen, Denken, Handeln: How the Brain Controls Our Behavior* (2001), Professor Gerhard Roth describes how the human brain functions, leading to action via emotions and thoughts. In an article published by *Deutschlandfunk*, the author, Matthias Eckoldt remarks that Roth's work should actually be called "Fühlen, Denken, Fühlen, Handeln" (Feeling, Thinking, Sensing, Acting). He justifies his suggestion with Roth's statements that the limbic system of the human brain, which is responsible for emotions, has the first and the last word in decisions related to the execution of actions.

To illustrate this with an example: A dangerous animal sprints towards a human being. The latter first reacts on the basis of his experiences, which make it clear to him that it is a dangerous situation. The first thing that comes up, is not the thought of what animal it is and whether it is white with orange stripes, or orange with white stripes. Instead, fear immediately shoots into his consciousness, from which the first reactions of the human body occur; the pulse and breathing accelerate to increase the oxygen supply and prepare for escape. In this extreme situation, the feelings are so dominant that thoughts – that is, reason and the use of one's knowledge – do not come into play at all. Instead, the feeling of fear dominates, and flight is chosen. This confirms Roth's assertion that feelings have the last word.

On the other hand, let's take another situation that is less extreme: The alarm clock rings at 5 a.m. Anke L. has no desire to get up. The desire for comfort, contentment, a sense of well-being and other pleasant feelings would be responsible for turning off the alarm clock and continuing to sleep. But Anke L. has, if she is not too sleepy, the opportunity and time to use her reason. She decides to defy her feelings based on valid arguments (e.g., going to work, taking children to school). However, she cannot help but notice, that while she is defying these feelings, they are still present and want to persuade her to go back to bed and continue sleeping. Again, Roth's assertion is confirmed: although the person makes a decision contrary to her feelings, the feelings are present both before and after the decision.

In every situation in which you fight your feelings with reason, try to observe how strong the power of your feelings is. It is different for each person. Some people are even able to put their feelings aside completely. These people are usually called disciplined. Other people have to fight harder against what is popularly called the "inner pig dog".

Did you know?

The cerebrum accounts for 85% of the total brain mass. It is surrounded by the cerebral cortex. This is also referred to as the cortex. The neocortex has the highest share of the cortex, at 90%.

It has developed during the course of the evolution of the human sensory organs. Among other things, the limbic system is located here, which controls the development of emotions, and drives behavior, as well as the release of some hormones. It has been proven that signals from the outside world are first processed in the limbic system. Only further processing in the upstream brain regions, which are decisive for the formation of the human mind, leads to a balancing of the emotional and rational aspects. This is how humans arrive at their actions – first via emotions and then via thoughts.

Knowledge about the physiological processes in the brain explains why thoughts and feelings play such an important role in determining actions. But why the feelings with certain persons in certain situation, come to bear and gives way to reason, isn't answered. Here other components must be included, which are revealed with a deeper look at the human consciousness.

Subconscious: Deep anchoring of beliefs

Placebos. Placebo. Deception. When a placebo works, it achieves a desired effect without administering a drug that would normally be necessary. It is a placebo without any efficacy. And yet it works: If a patient is in pain and is administered a placebo without knowing that it is one, the patient's expectation of efficacy sometimes produces the intended effect. It relieves pain or otherwise contributes to improvement in some patients, even though it is not supposed to do so. The medical reason for this is that the patient's expectations and accompanying beliefs cause them to release hormones that reduce pain.

Research has found that the body already releases dopamine and endogenous opioids at the level of the spinal cord to relieve pain. In research done in the 1970s, it was recognized that after the placebo effect had occurred, the administration of an opioid antagonist (an agent that inhibits the release of opioids; note) inhibited the placebo effect.

Man is able to initiate corresponding processes in the body just by believing in an effect. This impression is reinforced by the fact that, in addition to placebos, there are also nocebos. Nocebos are medications that contain an active ingredient but do not produce the intended effect.

Why do things sometimes go one way, sometimes another? Why does one body respond to medication, but not the other? In some cases, there are medical reasons. They can be non-responders for various reasons: The body simply does not respond to the respective active ingredient because, for example, it lacks enzymes, or because a (further) disease prevents it. But nocebos would not be called nocebos if they could be explained by the facts just described. One speaks of nocebos only if the drug should work on the respective person but does not. Science is in the habit of giving a name to phenomena. The cause of these phenomena probably lies in the place where you also develop positive habits in your thoughts: the subconscious.

What is the subconscious mind? Does it even exist?

There are few scientifically reliable statements about the human subconscious. In contrast to the limbic system, which can be measured by hormone release, the subconscious is a kind of mystery. The question arises whether the subconscious even exists.

26

Modern cognitive psychology and brain research describes the subconscious, in short, as an accumulation of processes in the brain that take place so quickly that only the results of thoughts become conscious, but not the individual steps that led to the results, such as a certain action or the pronunciation of certain words. According to the theory, the background of the subconscious is automation processes within the human brain, which serve to reduce energy consumption and simplify thought processes. There is also the theory of Sigmund Freud, who connects the subconscious with repressed drive representations.

This book follows the thesis of modern cognitive psychology and brain research, which describes the subconscious mind as rapidly running processes. This thesis is now contrasted with the theories of scientists who believe that there is no subconscious. The facts are as follows: No, there is no subconscious that can be clearly located in the brain and proven by means of measurements; at least not according to the current state of research. There is no clear proof that subconscious processes take place, which is widely criticized by researchers. Professor Nick Chater of the British Warwick Business School, for example, points to the lack of evidence for an existing subconscious. There is no evidence that, while we are thinking about one thing, other thought processes are going on somewhere inside us, Chater says. This is the radical view of a science that dwells only on solid evidence.

Now please think about the following situations and judge for yourself whether there might be some form of subconsciousness after all:

> ➢ Have you ever made your way to school, university, work, a friend's house, or another frequently visited place without having to think about the route?
> ➢ Have you ever succeeded in instinctively giving a correct answer to a question even though you were mentally absent?
> ➢ Have you succeeded in movements or workflows without thinking about them in more detail?

One of these cases has certainly occurred before in your life. We call them automatisms: The human being performs something frequently; knows it off the top of his head. Which is why he masters the correct execution right away, regardless of whether he is currently mentally present or not.

Now the bow is drawn to the pessimists and optimists of the world, who steer their thoughts in a negative or positive direction by force of habit. It is noticeable that some people are gifted in seeing disadvantages in all things. They almost automatically have a negative basic attitude no matter how desirable a positive attitude could be. Observe this best with yourself or in your circle of acquaintances. How many people maintain a positive approach and in which circumstances, and how many tend to be more negative?

There is no subconscious that can be anatomically or physiologically located in the brain as functionally demonstrated. But the subconscious exists as a term for processes and basic attitudes that are deeply rooted in us. Nocebos, placebos, optimistically and pessimistically attuned people, automated flawless actions with simultaneous mental absence and many other occurrences are proof to the existence of a kind of consciousness that lies hidden deep within us and that controls us to some extent. Therefore, the subconscious also controls success somehow too.

Did you know?

Few scientists dare to look for scientifically tenable explanations as to how the subconscious could contribute to an improvement in external circumstances through a positive basic attitude. The idea that one can influence the environment through positive thoughts seems too romantic. One, at least interesting effort, is that of Dr. Ulrich Warnke, who assesses the influencing of the immediate environment with physical forces. Allegedly, the nerves and muscles responsible for speech and action contribute to the creation of action potentials. It is known that through the brain – and the thoughts and mind that control it – signals are sent through the body to cause movements of the mouth when talking, or other parts of the body during other activities. Molecules have an elementary function in this process, he said. Molecules are composed of protein compounds that are influenced and changed by the mind. Besides, it is certain that the molecule connections are influenced by electrons which have a certain rotation – called "spin". Just like the molecular compounds, spin would be influenced by consciousness and thoughts. Because the energy of the human being could work outward, it is a certainty for Warnke that the human being influences matter outside of his body through the mind.

Scientific theses such as those of Dr. Ulrich Warnke venture into a field that attempts to fathom the effect of a possibly existing subconscious, by means of logical and known physical processes. First of all, there is the realization that there is something slumbering in man that influences his thoughts and actions. It works conspicuously fast and far away from our control; automated if you will. It was given the name subconscious. The existence of numerous best-sellers and the methodologies of respected psychologists speak for the fact that the subconscious exists. They are the key to learning how to trim the subconscious for success.

Rearrange the subconscious mind: Why? How? With what?

Assuming the thesis that the conversion of the subconscious mind is synonymous with the creation of a certain basic attitude towards life – how can this thesis be consolidated? The answer, because the subconscious mind refers to a set of automated processes in the brain, it can be called the place where basic human attitudes are hidden. A person who thinks exclusively and automatically negatively is characterized by a negative basic attitude. If in one's own subconscious mind, which is obviously negatively attuned, a positive mindset were to lie dormant, the result would be that the person would have a positive basic attitude and would increase the probability of achieving success.

Too complicated? Then here it is again in the simple version:

➢ If we increasingly think negatively and look for something negative in every circumstance or "paint the devil on the wall" so to speak, then we automate the brain to always take a negative viewpoint.

> ➤ Since we are talking about automated thought processes, we can assume a deep rooting of negative views, which leads us to the subconscious.
>
> ➤ Switching the subconscious mind would result in automated positive thought patterns.
>
> ➤ Since thoughts and feelings lead to actions, and a positive automation of them directs actions in a positive, safe, and successful direction, a conversion of the subconscious mind is purposeful.

Thus, by changing the subconscious mind, one replaces, step by step, the negative, or non-target beliefs with positive or target ones. This is how you get closer to success. Success habit "positive thoughts" is the first step in the formation of positive habits in the aim of becoming a successful person. The challenge with this first step is that what is programmed in the subconscious mind is deeply rooted.

Accordingly, the question is how and with what, can you change your subconscious mind? The solution to this riddle is: forming positive habits in relation to thoughts. For this purpose, there are several beliefs and exercises, with which the thoughts are reprogrammed. Anyway: enough of theory, and into practice!

Positive basic attitude through a positive subconscious: The practice phase

In connection with a positive conversion of the subconscious, one model is better known than almost any other: the law of attraction. It is said that this law is a principle known for thousands of years. Rhonda Byrne writes in her world-famous bestseller *The Secret* even before the table of contents:

> *"As above, so below.*
> *As inside, so outside."*

She locates this quotation on an emerald tablet dating to the third millennium BC. If you are looking for further evidence, you will find it in the Bible:

> *"Therefore, I say to you: Whatever you pray for and ask, believe that you have received it, and it will be given to you."* – Mark 11:24

In addition, there are the many works by successful people and other doers, who cite the law of attraction as the key to personal success. For example, T. Harv Ecker formulates in his successful work *So denken Millionäre* (2006) that the "subconscious financial behavior pattern" is the core factor that determines whether all learning, knowledge and all activities produce change. According to this, the occurrence of success is dependent on the correct programming of the subconscious mind.

These examples should make it clear that nothing is taken out of the air, but that the model is rather world-famous – apparently since several millennia! But what does this model, demand from you at all? What must be done so that it works in your favor?

The Law of Attraction requires you to think positively in every way: in terms of money, your dreams, family, career, and everything else in your life, you are to think in such a way that you steer success in your direction. Whenever a task or challenge comes up, you are not to think about the obstacles and adversities. The focus should be on your personal abilities and belief in success. Getting into the habit of this automated positive mindset – this is exactly what the Law of Attraction requires. The fact that this habit is anything but simple is already revealed to you by the previous contents in this book about the functioning of the brain and the subconscious. New automatisms must be developed, which requires exercises. These exact exercises are presented below to help you magnetically attract success, happiness and all other important objectives.

The following examples provide an impression of what is possible:

> **Occupation:** You are in sales. Product-selling is hard at the moment. The reasons lie in the market, in the target group and in certain features of the product that are difficult to market. But you are an optimist! You are used to always thinking and acting as if you sold the product to the last customer and had a remarkable run. Even if you were not successful with a hundred customers before, you only think about success anyway. Because in your world of thought you have already sold umpteen products and are a doer!

> *Is that unrealistic? Is this way of thinking unwise? If you are in product development, yes. But if you have no influence on product*

improvements and are only responsible for sales, then you have to make the best out of what you currently have at this point. In this case, the best way to act is to approach each customer with optimism, friendliness, and the confidence of having made many sales. At some point you will really sell the products because your attraction will not allow you to do otherwise.

➢ **Love life:** There she / he walks by. The woman / man of your dreams. Love at first sight is only a few steps away. But you yourself have always been shy. Now you happen to have the right topic ready to start a conversation. But there are doubts because you have never approached the opposite sex with confidence. Fortunately, your recent reading has taught you what's important: that you don't think about your past history at all in this situation. You create for yourself the thoughts of a person who can approach others and seize opportunities. That's how you do it, and before you know it you've already made a sympathetic start to the conversation with that confident smile and a bright, calm, yet fun-loving "hello." The rest will take care of itself...

Is this scenario unrealistic? A person who was completely despondent now proactively approaches another; the opposite sex at that? In fact, a positive approach ensures that the positivity will be reciprocated. If you approach the apparent love of your life confidently and sympathetically, you can expect a similar response, whereupon you gain even more confidence. If, on the other hand, you yell at the person to get over your subconscious dominant insecurity, then of course many things might go wrong. In this example, there is no guarantee of you immediately following in Casanova's footsteps and succeeding at everything interpersonally. But you will increase your probability of success and the probability of a string of positive experiences with a positive mindset.

➢ **Exams / Competitions:** Negative thoughts are distracting because they worry you. Calculating, reasoning, or completing the exam task under pressure requires a clear and focused mind. A subconsciously programmed mind that says, "I can do it!" Will leave you hungry for exam tasks so that you will continue to put in an excellent performance. The same is true for competitions: if you know you will make it because there is no alternative in your mind, you will hit the golf ball with greater conviction and get significantly closer to the hole than if you hit it tentatively and with uncertainty.

Now sports, too! Does the law not stop at any area of life? No, because the way one approaches any matter shapes the way one performs. Success is more likely to occur with a convinced approach, because full attention without worries and negative thoughts serves the purpose of contributing one's own competences and abilities in the best possible way.

Lesson 1: Avoid negations

This first lesson will lead you to become aware of your goals, to record them, and to record them *correctly*. For now, it doesn't matter whether you have big or small goals: write down everything you can think of about them. These can be vague statements like, "I want to take more time for certain things." or concrete statements like, "I want to be a millionaire by the time I'm 35." In the beginning, you just collect what's on your mind; long-term as well as short-term goals are welcome. If you are unsure of what you want, sit down and think about where you are in your life. Set realistic goals that are achievable using the resources available to you at the desired time. Keep your goals in small steps or stages so that you can see your progress more quickly.

Up to this point, it is usually still quite simple. If all of your goals are not yet clear, at least some already are. Some classics among the goals are a successful diet, a higher income, a life partner, living out hobbies and regular travel. Where it gets significantly harder, however, is in the formulation of goals, wishes and dreams. The mistake that most people make is based on the subconscious negative attitude that they have become accustomed to in part or in full. It manifests itself in thinking in negations:

- ➢ "I don't want to get a bad grade."
- ➢ "I don't want to embarrass myself."
- ➢ "I don't want to fail."
- ➢ "I'm not afraid."

Task 1

Read through each of the sentences in the list and let each one sink in for a while. Try to notice what images are created in your mind by each sentence. Select other sentences in which the words "not" or "none" are used. What images do these sentences evoke in your mind?

If you couldn't find a concrete solution to the problem, it doesn't matter. However, thinking about it is the first important step in understanding the problem. The fact that you may not have had a concrete thought from the sentences or that no image appeared, is because many such sentences do not actively encourage a concrete image. They merely deny one thing, while leaving millions of other things still conceivable. To derive a concrete and purposeful, positive message from them is almost impossible in these cases. But it is much more likely that the negative message gets through to the brain because the brain cannot process negations. In formulations such as "no fear," "don't fail," or "don't get a bad grade," the negation is prefixed, but what is the brain more likely to perceive – the negating addendum – or the particular cue (e.g., fear, failure) that is associated with emotions based on previous experiences in life? The answer is – more likely the latter.

Did you know?

Despite a lack of scientifically robust evidence on the effect of negative wording, various professional and personal groups assume that it should be avoided in order to achieve a goal. In sales psychology it is taught not to use words like "problem" at all, even if it is "no problem". These are alarm words that immediately leave a negative impact in the subconscious. Doctors who want to be a support for their patients in serious illnesses often speak of the survival rates of certain treatments instead of mortality rates.

An important point was already revealed in the box: There is little to no scientifically reliable evidence for the effect or non-effect of negative formulations. The observations from several decades of psychology, behavioral research, marketing and other disciplines are almost the only resilient theses. The amount of advocates to build on positive formulations instead of negative formulations is meanwhile overwhelming; so overwhelming that even in science a little bit is happening. Andrea Birchler writes in her thesis on the role of positive and negative suggestions in anesthesia induction (2018), citing several scientific sources, that positive suggestions may well lead to a reduction in numerous complaints in patients after surgical procedures. A logical explanation for the "non-effect" of negations can certainly be discerned in the functions of the brain, putting the whole thesis on a more solid footing: While the left hemisphere of the brain processes logical connections, the right hemisphere is responsible for processing life events. The right hemisphere of the brain works faster. Thus, when the negation "do not fail" is thought or uttered, the image of failure is first generated because it is associated with events that one has experienced oneself. The later connection with the "negation" subsequently plays only a subordinate role.

Task 2

Focus on positive phrases. Replace all goals, wishes, and other desires on your list, if phrased negatively, with positive phrases. For example, "I don't want to live alone," becomes "I'll find a partner." Let's go!

It is not easy to switch from the negative to the positive if you have been used to "painting the devil on the wall" for several years or decades. If it is difficult for you, then at the end of this first lesson there is still a realization that should give you great courage: Everything negative has a positive antithesis. This positive contrast is not as far away as you might think. Because it is on the same scale.

Fear ---

Doubt ------------------------------------

Lack of Self Confidence ------------------------

Lack of Optimism ------------------------------------

Failure -------------------------------- *Success*

Task 3

Are you still looking for the appropriate positive keyword for your goal to replace the negation? Then start writing down the negative cues, and on the same line with some space in between, write down the positive opposites. In the space between, mark on a scale how far you are from the positive aspect. Then continue reading the book. After lesson 3 in the next but one section (after having done all the exercises) go back to the scale and assess whether anything has changed. Feel free to keep your personal scale for the long term to document how your beliefs evolve – ideally a little bit to the right each week; from fear to courage, from doubt to confidence, from pessimism to optimism, and so on for the many other scales you have found for yourself.

Lesson 2: Positive affirmations!

In principle, the word combination "positive affirmations" is doubled, because affirmations are positive by nature. They are doubled for stylistic reasons to emphasize the importance of this topic. Affirmations are used to describe a state or situation – always as good, always as positive. With affirmations, there is no longer any talk of set goals or formulated wishes. If one applies affirmations, one imagines having already achieved something:

➢ "I'm wealthy."
➢ "I have an attractive body."

> ➤ "I got a very good grade."
> ➤ "I landed the deal."

While the first two example sentences refer to general and longer states, the last two apply to individual events (a grade from an exam, a result from a negotiation). In affirmations, these events are in the future. One wants to feel confident and courageous for a future event by suggesting to one's subconscious that it has already taken place with success. Accordingly, affirmations refer to both actual and target states. However, one always speaks and thinks as if one had already achieved one's goal or dream.

Task 1

Think about the advantages and disadvantages of telling your subconscious mind that you have already reached your goal, even though this is not (yet) the case. After all, this is what affirmations demand. From this, deduce in which situations it would make the most sense to make use of affirmations, and when it would be better to proceed with caution. Write down your thoughts on a piece of paper.

Affirmations like the belief that you have already achieved something, increase the danger of carelessness (perhaps you have already noted this). After all, when something is achieved, you can rest on your laurels – can't you? It's a bit of a character issue, but the general risk is there. Interestingly, there are several robust studies on the effect of affirmations, that say the risk is outweighed by the added value. Emily Falk of the *University of Pennsylvania* in Philadelphia conducted one such study with 46 subjects. The results were measured with functional magnetic resonance imaging (fMRI). One particular part of the study focused on self-affirmation. It found that when a person tells himself several times that he is helpful, self-confident, disciplined or ascribes other such positive character traits, it changes his attitude and shapes his character. Applying the findings of this study, it may not be advisable to ascribe to yourself that you have already landed a deal, won a competition or achieved some other goal straight away, because this could still lead to carelessness in preparation for the event. But ascribing general positive qualities or characteristics to yourself can be a sustainable way to enhance your self-image.

Task 2

You could go far enough out on a limb as to say then, that positive affirmations about yourself are definitely beneficial. Therefore, I recommend using them to steer your character in a direction that is conducive to your goals. For example, if you have the goal of getting rid of your closed-mindedness to new experiences (e.g., trying different recreational activities, foods, and / or styles of clothing), set goal-directed affirmations: "I like to try X." If you want to give this a stronger foundation, make further use of a rationale: "I like trying X because I recently had Y [insert positive experience]." Write down any affirmations you want to use.

This guidebook would be only half as helpful if it dealt exclusively with the positive sides of each theory. Therefore, it must be admitted, that there is also scientific counter evidence regarding the added value of affirmations. A study by Wood, Perunovic et al. (2009) showed that, among test subjects, those most in need of the effects of affirmations could benefit the least from them. The affirmations could possibly even do harm because the subjects naturally looked for counter evidence, and easily found it. There-fore, the researchers involved in the study recommended that af-firmations be used "moderately." So instead of using overly comprehensive and euphoric phrases such as "I have a fantastic body," moderating it to "I have made good progress with my body" should be preferred.

Because the benefits of affirmations are there, but the critical voices also have their justification, it is recommended that you find your own golden mean. You should not make yourself be-lieve that you have already successfully overcome upcoming events. This distorts reality. Also, you should not put yourself in a euphoric light within the framework of general affirmations. Make sure that you encourage yourself and tell yourself that you are getting closer to your goals. But leave the affirmations open to the fact that you still see room for improvement and will continue to work towards the goals.

Task 3

Consider the affirmations you formulated in Task 2 and revise them so that they are more moderate. Everything that follows is pure practice: Take 3 to 5 minutes at a time, several times a day, to talk positively to yourself. Say the affirmations out loud. You could stand in front of a mirror and make an optimistic facial ex-pression. Alternatively, you could sit down and think the affirma-tions with a high level of concentration. Do not jump from one affirmation to another but do use every break in the day for an-other affirmation. The more often you do these affirmation exer-cises, the more the positive beliefs will anchor themselves into your subconscious mind.

Lesson 3: Visualizations with strength!

To visualize something means to see it – regardless of whether it is there or not. If you remember your school days or have had experience with lectures in your job, you will surely know how important visualizations are: A lecture where only speaking is done is less interesting than a lecture where additional pictures, graphics, videos and more are shown. Nowadays in marketing, the importance of visualization is also enormous. Influencers on social media increasingly work with infographics, and even top companies make use of animated films or other media. Visualization has the important property of communicating complex issues in a simple way. Consequently, the conveyed content remains better in the memory, consciousness and even subconscious. It is exactly these advantages of visualization that you can make use of to penetrate your subconscious mind more concisely with positive beliefs.

Task 1

Consider what types of visualizations might apply to the beliefs you wrote down in the first 2 lessons. Imagine both mental and physical visualization possibilities, using various objects and materials.

Successful people are said to be gifted in the field of visualization. An ideal example of this, which Rhonda Byrne also cites in her work *The Secret* (2007), is inventors. The Wright brothers with the airplane, Thomas Edison with the light bulb, Alexander Graham Bell with the telephone – according to the author, all these inventions could not have been created if the inventors had not had a picture in front of their eyes. Even nowadays at major corporations, such as Apple and Microsoft, designs are first recorded and visualized using graphics programs before they are physically implemented in the products.

Did you know?

83% of information is absorbed through the eye. For some time now, companies have been making use of this insight in brand psychology. According to Florack, Scarabis et al. (2012), the eye is the most dominant sensory organ in human perception. Contexts are answered faster because more brain regions are involved. The effect of images on the brain becomes even stronger if they convey emotions. As findings by Müller, Andersen et al. (2011) show: Measuring brain waves in subjects showed that an emotional stimulus intensified the effect of the images to such an extent that patients were distracted even when they had previously been highly concentrated.

Visualizations are a decisive factor on the road to success. Without visualizations, a considerable amount of innovations and successes would not exist. However, based on scientific research, it is becoming apparent that the goal should be to stimulate emotions in the course of visualizations. This is apparently how the greatest effectiveness on the human brain is achieved, leading to penetration deep into the subconscious. All this evidence raises the question of the appropriate methods of visualization: *How do you manage to create visualizations in relation to your goals and desires that leave a lasting impression on the subconscious due to the emotional impact?*

➢ Bringing movement into the performances.
➢ Encourage imagination through music.

- ➢ Design images.
- ➢ Create vision boards.
- ➢ Use software.

Because not every person has the desire, time or skill to tinker, we will first describe a simple method of visualization that is feasible for you in any case: your own imagination. Take the goals and desires that you want to visualize and imagine how you will achieve them. This is how simple this first method is. Practice makes perfect, so in the long run you will be able to visualize without much preparation. In the short term, however – especially if you're doing it for the first time – you should create an appropriate backdrop for visualization. Ideally, this setting should be quiet, comfortable, and free from disturbance for at least 5 to 10 minutes; for example, any room in your home: You can visualize in the bathtub, in bed after waking up (this is a good morning ritual as long as you don't fall asleep right away), in the living room, in an armchair or in other similar places. It is also good to visualize outside on a park bench. If it suits you, you can encourage relaxation by lighting a candle or something. Most importantly, take your time and clear your mind of negative thoughts. Get yourself to the destination of your dreams and feel your success!

My experience

I was helped enormously by visualizations before my contracts. Before I started with visualizations, I always had a strong aversion to a lecture. I projected negative experience onto new listeners I didn't even know yet, and I went into the lecture with a negative basic attitude. Inspired by the fact that I had kept order in other areas of my life, been disciplined on my days off, and had cultivated a general zest for life, I decided to approach the lectures positively too. For this, I created images in my mind of the best lectures I had ever given. I closed my eyes for 5 minutes before each lecture, and imagined the people's laughter, the high-level conversations, the interest of the audience, and the pleasant breaks we spent together loosely. Then, I went into the lectures in a more positive mood and was able to cope relatively well, even with the lectures that normally would have gone completely wrong.

Just the thought of success can help you. To promote effective visualization in your mind, here are two tools from a previous list: exercise and music. Rhonda Byrne in her cited work, referring to the experiences of Dr. John Demartini, points out the problems associated with static visualization: It can easily collapse in on itself. Bringing movement into a visualization can help you to avoid this, as it creates a dynamic that makes it easier for you to break away from negative beliefs that may still be present. For example, you could visualize the entire process from the present moment until you reach your goal. In this way you would see a small movie with intermediate stages, and ups and downs, as well as the deserved reward at the end. The second method that will help you to visualize, is choosing appropriate music. Music can accompany both static visualizations, and inner movies. Despite the specificity of music tastes, some artists, bands or certain tracks are considered to be more optimal motivational music in helping you achieve your goals. Here is a small track list for inspiration with 5 instrumentals and 5 (more exotic) songs:

➢ Two Steps from Hell – Heart of Courage

- Hans zimmer – time
- Emancipator – minor cause
- Steve Jablonsky – My Name is Lincoln
- Brad fiedel – terminator 2 main theme
- Eminem – Lose yourself
- Survivor – Eye of the Tiger
- Queen – We are the Champions
- T. I. – live your life
- College feat. Electric Youth – A real Hero

With time you will probably find your own tracks or maybe learn to love these ones too. In general, it has been shown that motivational songs usually develop their best effect sonically and in "epic" versions. Thus, visualizations become maximally convincing through moving images, movies in front of the inner eye, dynamics and music in your own imagination.

Task 2

It's time to activate your imagination. On the one hand, you have learned about visualization through imagination in an appropriate environment. On the other hand, you know how to underline the visualization with dynamic scenarios in your thought processes, as well as with the right music. Practice makes perfect, so try yourself out in a one-week practice phase: Take time at a preferred moment each day to do the visualization on your own terms. Whenever and however, you do it: do it right and don't underestimate the power of small details! You are welcome to continue reading the contents of this book during the week of practice and complete the next exercises in parallel.

The inner, mental visualization can be supported or replaced with external tools: The creation and use of images and vision boards, as well as special software, are good options for this. It sounds like sophisticated art, but in a way it is banal. Cut a photo of your role model from a magazine and replace its head with yours. Take a pinboard to which you pin pictures of your intended success and milestones. Use special software to create your own movies and insert pictures of yourself. Strictly speaking, you don't even have to pin your pictures anywhere. If you really appreciate a person as your role model, even photos of this person on a pinboard are enough to achieve the visualization effect. The advantage of this external visualization, which does not only take place in your own imagination, is that you are regularly confronted with your goals by simply looking at the pinboard or watching the movie.

Task 3

Choose at least one method of physical visualization and design it. It is enough to pin 2 or 3 pictures of yourself reaching the goal on a wall. For visualization software, you are welcome to check out *Mind Movies*. Add at least one physical visualization method to the mental visualization from Task 2. Keep the physical visualization for the long term. The advantage being that, once created, you can look at pictures, boards and movies at any time thereafter. Take the opportunity to look at your visualization regularly during the day or week.

Lesson 4: Rethinking your own views

So far, work has been done on the emotional side; the habits of not thinking in negations, repeating affirmations moderately and consciously, and making use of visualizations serve the emotional side. If you think automatically about positive things because you have learned this through habits, the positive emotions are activated directly along with it. But the brain doesn't only work according to emotions and automated thought processes. As you have already learned, after the emotional part, further brain regions switch on, which are classified in the vernacular as reason, understanding, the rational side, intelligence etc.

It's about you being able to exert thought processes that no longer just follow emotions. These thought processes are not automated but are actually controlled by yourself. If you are a person who is generally less controlled by emotions, lessons 1 to 3 will possibly help you only a little. For what is the use of an automated positive thought, if you then only have eyes for the negative arguments in your mind and – driven by these – decide to approach a matter pessimistically or without confidence anyway?

An example of what has been described up to this point: A very good friend who has had a lot of success in his life comes back to the city where you live after several years. Both of you are happy to see each other again. The friend, who is very wealthy, wants to start a business with you. Your first thoughts are automatically positive – after all the hours of visualizations and affirmations, that's probably the least you can do. But as soon as your friend says goodbye, you begin to brood in the evening. The shad-

ows of moonlight settle over the enthusiastic initial thought processes. You weigh argumentatively how many people have already
been betrayed by friends, that you haven't seen your friend for a
long time and that he might want to harm you... Whether these
thoughts are right or not doesn't matter at this point. The point
of the example was only to show that automated thoughts or feelings focused on success are not everything. It is also important to
direct your rational arguments, your mind, and your other mental
competences in a positive direction. Please don't misunderstand:
It's not about turning off critical thinking and having eyes only for
the positive aspects. This would be fatal under certain circumstances. You would miss valid arguments that speak against something. The aim of the following paragraph is merely to banish
unnecessary and all-overshadowing blackness from your
thoughts. In lesson 4 you should get used to reconsidering your
own views. Away from the always negative, towards the: *Maybe I
am overdoing it with my negative view and should start to take other perspectives as well?*

Notice

Taking on board other points of view, which is explored in
more detail in Lesson 5 (and can be deepened for challenging issues), is also a trump card that goes beyond getting used to positive thinking. As soon as you get used to taking on board other
people's points of view, you will find that you can direct the conversation much better and make it more successful. This will give
you new opportunities in professional, personal and other conversations. Being able to have nuanced conversations defines inter-
personal success and thus, in part, overall success.

What helps in order to consider other points of view is the so-called NLP (Neurolinguistic Programming). You will encounter it in several places in this book. Because what evergreens are for the music scene, NLP is for lay psychology in recent years. It is in demand in several industries, for example management. The article from WirtschaftsWoche *Marketing or Method? The dispute about neurological remote control* (2019) tries to evaluate the current importance of NLP. The NLP seminar market is flourishing; companies, managers and private individuals are booking seminars in rows to better analyze customers, applicants and fellow human beings. Nevertheless, the magazine, citing the views of scientists, emphasizes that NLP has several shortcomings. It presumes to make human behavior predictable and people manipulable.

Did you know?

NLP was developed by Richard Bandler and John Grinder in the 1970s. Both observed and analyzed the work of the most successful psychologists of the time in order to derive laws from it. NLP is based on certain assumptions, which are used to analyze communication processes. By means of instructions and advice, NLP helps to successfully shape communication processes. With the further development of NLP – over several generations – additional areas of application have been opened up. These include the development of positive habits, anxiety therapy, self-motivation and more.

Several theses of NLP have been refuted. The critics, however, demonize the entire model because of individual weaknesses, which is not fair. This is because NLP consists of a large number of assumptions, methods and mechanisms, not all of which are useful in life, but many of which are. Some of the more useful assumptions are:

> "The map is not the territory."
> "The best option available is always (unconsciously) chosen."
> "If one person can learn to do something, then in principle other people can too."

These three assumptions can be beneficial for your further path. You could get off to a good start with the first assumption, which means nothing other than that each person perceives the world differently. Politics, for example, is a popular topic of argument. What seems correct to you may seem completely wrong to another person. You and the other person have grown up under different conditions. This is one of the reasons for the different views. Mostly, the topic of politics is therefore avoided before it degenerates into an argument. But a discussion with openness for the opinion of others and a rational consideration without including personal emotions, can actually be purposeful for both parties. Perhaps both would learn something? So, it is important in human relationships to develop openness to other points of view, insofar as it enriches you with new and differentiated knowledge.

The second basic assumption leads you to the statement that man always chooses the method which subjectively seems to be the most meaningful to him. Exactly here a problem arises: What is subjectively best is not automatically actually so. These objective considerations are of great importance, and NLP helps you to get used to developing several choices in your mind, which do not only follow subjective, emotional and subconscious criteria.

The third basic assumption from the list serves as motivation. It says that if others can learn something, you can learn it too. It is not meant to say that every person finds it equally easy or difficult to learn a certain thing. It is only pointing out the fact that, in principle, every person can learn a specific thing.

Task 1

Sit down quietly and take at least half an hour. Think back to the last 5 to 10 conflicts you had; whether they were internal conflicts with yourself or conflicts with other people doesn't matter. Show yourself to be open to other points of view by considering whether you really went about it the right way. Should you have been more open to an argument? With time, you will notice that it is easier for you to judge less emotionally.

There is nothing wrong with reacting instinctively, as long as you don't let it blind you. The goal in this fourth lesson is to reduce your emotions. If you learned to think positive automatically in the first 3 lessons, it was still beneficial. This is because a positive initial reaction will make you more willing to deal with an issue and approach it with maximum confidence. So, since you'll never be able to completely suppress emotions, you've done an important job. Now the goal is for you to get used to turning on your mind more quickly in order to weigh arguments clearly and make the objectively right decisions.

Task 2

Begin this task by conditioning yourself to control your emotions. Several mechanisms exist to help you do this, including affirmations again: Try to convince yourself that you are in control of your emotions. Eventually this will enter your subconscious mind. Possible affirmations are "I am absolutely in control," and "I am a very calm person."

Supplement these affirmations with regular breathing exercises and meditations. Even if this is not your thing; just do it. Do it for a few minutes a day for 1 or 2 weeks. Because even if you don't like the exercise, it has already helped many people achieve their goals. Success-proven exercises should always be done consistently if you are serious about your goal.

Also, expose yourself more often to situations in which it is difficult for you to control your emotions. These situations can be acted out with other people. The confrontation will toughen you up. Alternatively, you can determine an inconspicuous finger gesture that you make whenever you are overcome by emotions. This gesture serves as a signal for you to calm down. With regular practice, you get used to holding back emotions. This is beneficial for negative emotions, but also for exuberant positive emotions.

Now the only thing left to do is to let the withheld emotions be followed by rational arguments. NLP comes into play at this point. It helps you to take a different perspective. This applies to conversations with other people as well as to your own thought processes in order to master inner conflicts. For this purpose, three methods of NLP will now be presented to you.

> **Dissociation**: Inner conflict with yourself? Then imagine that you are not affected by it, but that another person is in your place. Sit down, close your eyes, and imagine a movie playing before you. See yourself in this movie as if you were watching another person. What would you say

about this person's thoughts and actions? Good or bad? Through dissociation, the problem is no longer bound to you, but becomes unbound from you. So, you illuminate the problems as an outsider and gather more objective arguments.

➤ **Filter change**: When you talk to another person, take their perspective. Use different filters: What culture is the person from? How did the person grow up? How does the person feel today? What challenges has the person had to overcome in his life? Gather as much information as you can about a person and look at each topic of conversation from their point of view. You don't have to go off the deep end the first time you talk and make bold statements that might hurt the person. Get into the habit of being confident in your conversations but avoiding sensitive topics or remaining neutral, so that you can get their perspective first. In this way, you will be able to talk to them without hurting their feelings or questioning their view of the world.

➤ **Meta-model**: The meta-model of language states that people represent certain facts contrary to reality through language. The same happens in thoughts. That is why NLP encourages us to question these facts with regard to the following three aspects: erasure, generalization, distortion. Erasure is the representation of a fact with the omission of important clues. Generalization means a generalization of the facts. And distortion means formulating things differently than they really are. All three mechanisms can be used by people in thoughts against themselves, to deny a truth they do not want. Likewise, it is possible for a person to use this against another person in conversation. Therefore, arguments should be questioned: Are any of these three patterns of behavior present? Get into the habit of questioning your actions when making important personal decisions if you are not absolutely sure you are doing the right thing.

The application of these 3 methods from NLP is a long-term task for you. It is not about questioning yourself in every little thing or illuminating every little issue. But because thoughts in interaction with emotions lead to successful action and are characterized by sustainable and well-considered decisions, you should get used to using the ability of objective consideration. These methods of NLP and all the other lessons of the chapter so far will help you to do that.

Lesson 5: Pro and Con Lists for Challenging Issues

Decision trees, Benjamin Franklin lists, decision mind maps – the world is now full of visualization methods designed to simplify decisions and make them as correct as possible. No visualization method is simpler than the pros and cons list. Get into the habit of choosing it as a decision-making tool when:

1. You have the time to think about one thing for at least an hour.
2. You find a decision particularly difficult.
3. Multiple parties, and their perspectives, are involved in your decision.
4. The issue you have to decide on is complicated in different respects.

Pro and con lists are used for visualization. Advantages and disadvantages of a decision are compared with each other. This is done by means of a design element that every person is familiar with: a table. One column contains the advantages, the other the disadvantages. Line by line from top to bottom, one advantage and one disadvantage is listed. By writing down your thoughts, you make sure that no important aspect is forgotten. This risk would be present if you were to think about a decision without writing it down. Writing down your thoughts collects the arguments. It is advisable to extend the creation of a pros and cons list over several hours or days and to do something else in between. As you go about your daily life, new arguments will come to mind over time, so your pros and cons list will become more and more detailed.

Notice

In addition to simply listing the advantages and disadvantages, it is also helpful to weigh them. If you want to be especially accurate and maximize the likelihood of optimal decisions, then you should determine some categories with which you give a weighting to each argument. This way, arguments that are more influential will receive the necessary attention. In issues where only you are concerned, it is important to take into account the emotional aspect. After all, we humans are not robots...

You have learned to think in a differentiated way. This competence will benefit you especially in lists of pros and cons. You will increase the probability of proceeding correctly when making decisions about difficult issues. You will find a wealth of arguments and thus no longer disregard any aspect. Emotions will play less of a role, instead you will decide according to objective criteria in a way that is best for you and other people involved. This will bring you closer to your success – pro and con lists as a habit of success when making decisions.

However, challenges can arise with these acquired competencies. Because when you compile a large number of arguments, by considering a wide variety of viewpoints, you will end up with very long lists of pros and cons. Now the question arises how to bring clarity into all the arguments and make a decision.

The solution is to delete all pros and cons that are mutually exclusive and equally weighted. Example: You have noted a higher salary on the advantage side of a decision, and a higher expenditure of time on the disadvantage side. If available free time is as important to you as earnings, then these are two aspects that are equally weighted. Since the two aspects are mutually exclusive – you can only earn more in this example if you spend more time on it, so you cross out these advantages and disadvantages. In turn, you highlight the other arguments that are not mutually exclusive, to see if there is a preponderance on the side of advantages or disadvantages. The more advantages come up in the decision, the more likely you are to go for it.

Step 2: Change the habit of acting – identify meaning and determine correct habits

After the conversion of thoughts in the first step; in this chapter, it is time to act. Success is achieved through action. Whether possible actions are right or not, it will be dealt with in the third step.

This chapter is purely concerned with making sense of the new habitual action. The insights gained so far in this book, which include taking different perspectives from lesson 4 in the last chapter, will help you to do this. The goal is for you to be completely convinced that you will live better as a result of the changes in habit. Then you will develop what is essential for success: motivation and discipline.

Motivation and discipline - differences, role, connection

"Motivation refers to processes in which certain motives are activated and translated into actions. This gives behavior a direction toward a goal, a level of intensity, and a sequence of events. A person's motivation to pursue a particular goal depends on situational incentives, personal preferences, and their interaction." (Stangl, 2020).

If you understand change of habit as a process, you need motives to learn the new habit purposefully, intensively with consistency, and in a certain sequence. Without motives there is no motivation. To make motives as attractive as possible, there must be incentives that give you advantages in the situation and that are related to your desires.

"Discipline comes from Latin and stands for instruction, discipline and order. Discipline is the act of following rules or regulations. Self-control is referred to as self-discipline." (cf. Brockhaus 1988, p. 553; Stangl, 2020).

You want to develop new, positive habits that bring you success in some form of order. You create your personal idea of order. If you follow the accompanying rules for order and success, you will be self-disciplined and achieve your goals.

Motivation and discipline are two factors that help you make the transition. Motivation makes the change attractive for you, so that you *want to* change. Discipline, on the other hand, does not start with your desires or attractiveness. It is the strength to follow a certain goal, in a sense, *willpower*.

The following assertions can be made:

➤ You can still make a successful transition without discipline. In this case, it can be assumed that the motivation is so great that it surpasses the weakness of will.

➤ Without motivation, it is also possible to master the change. The assumption here is that your willpower is so great that you have a high level of resilience and still perform actions that do not suit you.

➤ *Without* motivation and discipline, you'll give up on a change after just a few days or even hours. You need at least one of the two components to persevere.

> ➤ With motivation *and* discipline together, it is easier to make the transition successfully.

> ➤ Discipline – or willpower – cannot be trained overnight. Mostly, a change of habit is about motivating yourself. Willpower is either present, absent, or occurs over time.

According to these explanations, the most important thing is that you first filter out the motives for the desired changes. You either have the discipline or you don't. To dwell on this point would be time-consuming. In the further course of this chapter, you will dedicate yourself to the motivation that arises from the fact that you recognize a sense or a motive in the change – at best even several motives.

Did you know?

As you get used to it, you may notice something fascinating that explains the connection between motivation, discipline, and habits. Namely, over time, routine replaces motivation and discipline. The more often you practice the new habit, the more likely it is to take root in your brain. You gain routine and have to exert less effort to comply with the habit you are striving for. Thus, the importance of motivation as well as discipline, to follow something, gradually decreases, until its importance is almost completely gone, and the routine drives the new habit so that you follow the actions automatically.

The motivation you need is temporary. There could hardly be more positive news for you because it follows that you will have to make less and less effort, during the transition, as time goes on. Although the need for motivation and discipline will increase in the first few days or weeks, this is only an initial phenomenon.

After overcoming a critical phase in which the changeover seems more difficult than at the beginning, the routine sets in, and it becomes constantly easier.

Lesson 1: Define success attractively and realistically for yourself

You are motivated when you set a desirable goal. You need, as you know since chapter 1, something that radiates attractiveness to you and awakens a desire in you. Then the emotions and thought processes play in your favor. Given the fact that you are reading this book, which relates habits and success, it is assumed that you want to become successful by changing your habits. Accordingly, your roughly formulated goal is success for now. In such a rough formulation, success sounds good, but nowhere near the level that you would find it attractive and strive for it with every fiber of your body. Yet that is exactly what you want to achieve; you must pine for what you define as a goal.

The destination can't be dictated to you, but the path by which you find a highly attractive destination can at least be shown to you. So, let's go: Practice says hello again!

A goal is more than just a word – paraphrase it!

When you formulate your goal, first make it precise with one word or one phrase. "Wealth" would be a phrase that is absolutely appropriate. Likewise, "family happiness" would be appropriate. "Graduated with an average grade of 1.0" also fits. One or the other goal may possibly leave more room for interpretation. This issue will be addressed later. First, exercise your senses to look at the respective goal from as multi-layered a perspective as possible – "multi-layered attractive" of course.

Task 1

You may remember your school lessons and the role of the 3 parts of speech: adjectives, verbs, and nouns. Adjectives describe what something is like – this is a good place to start! What the particular goal is may be formulated in one word. But what it is like to get there, to feel it, to enjoy it, to savor it, etc. is something else again. Therefore, write down all the adjectives that come to mind in connection with the goal you want to reach. If you don't have many ideas, feel free to use the wordassociations.net website, which will give you suggestions for adjectives that go with the word. For "wealth," some results would be "blessed," "intoxicating," and "influential," for example. It's also sometimes worth looking at similar verbs like "enjoy" and "marvel" in place of "wealth". Use this website, other websites, and your own imagination to paraphrase the goal attractively.

You may become rapt as you perform this task because you begin to feel your goal and enjoy its description. If you have ever felt an "exhilarating" state or have been "marveled at" by others, you will understand how desirable these states are. This will motivate you to realize your goal.

The goal, your success, is much more than just a word. You can look at the goal in so many ways that it becomes a shining image. And now comes a link with the first chapter: If you have already visualized the goal, you may now enrich the visualizations and other exercises with the images and ideas that this first task has generated in your mind. Make the goal as creative and appealing as possible!

Make fast progress real!

If you were assured that you would achieve your long-awaited goal in just one day, but in order to do so you would have to get up at 4 a.m. on that day, work for 12 hours, do 3 hours of sports, and study for 4 hours, you would not turn down the offer despite the high demand. Motivation is particularly high when big goals are achievable in an extraordinarily short time, or when the way to get there is easy.

This book cannot guarantee, that you will reach your big goal of success at lightning speed. It is also impossible to guarantee that it will be easy for you to reach the goal. But you probably already knew that. Nevertheless, this subchapter holds an important motivation for you, how to increase motivation by making use of a trick with which you "fool" your brain: the division of the goal into stages.

Several scientists believe that it makes sense to divide goals into stages. One of these scientists is psychology professor Wilhelm Hofmann from the University of Cologne. You will get to know him better in the next chapter as part of an experiment conducted in the documentary film *The Power of Habit*. The experiment from the film will provide you with several methods and tricks to help you with habits in the next chapter. Hofmann believes that changes of habit should be carried out using a clear strategy. Part of this strategy should be smaller stage goals.

The explanation for the benefit of stage goals is provided by an article in the ZEIT newspaper, which quotes the words of renowned brain researcher Gerhard Roth: "Instead of chasing after a big goal, you agree with yourself on small steps for which you think up equally small self-rewards." Increasing the intervals between the stage goals and lengthening the periods until the reward would additionally contribute to the changeover process, would eventually become automatic, and a new habit would develop.

So, the previous recommendations as targets for remapping are summarized step by step:

1. Define your big goal, and paraphrase it with adjectives, as well as other types of words, to make it attractive and linked with emotions.
2. Make goals even more attractive, through visualization methods and other means.
3. Make progress more visible and accelerate it through milestones.
4. Come up with rewards for individual stages, to increase motivation.
5. As the duration increases, increase the distance between the stages and the duration to the next reward.

Task 2

Proceed exactly as described in this sequence of steps with the major goals you have written down. For example, divide the goal "wealth" into several stages. You may assume that such a general word requires a particularly large number of stages. You can use account balances as stages. Alternatively, you are free to divide, according to the number of planned promotions, and the accompanying salary increase. Find your meaningful division in stages. Take plenty of time to do this. Set a reward for each stage. Make sure that the reward does not destroy the progress you have made so far. For example, after a week of successful dieting, having a fast-food day that resembles a "calorie escalation" would be counterproductive.

In particular, brain researcher Roth's recommendation to increase the distance between stages, and the duration until the next reward seems plausible, and is in line with the previous findings in this book. As motivation and discipline are increasingly replaced by the manifesting routine as the change progresses, rewards and the achievement of stage goals become less important. Eventually, the action gets into your blood and requires less incentive to implement.

Lesson 2: Find habits that bring success

Some habits exist that are universally conducive to success. "Universal" in this case means that they are beneficial regardless of your definition of success. To prove it, here is an example that was used several times in the first chapter, that is extremely understandable: a positive basic attitude towards life. The habit of thinking positively and optimistically is helpful when you:

- ➢ Want to lose weight.
- ➢ Are going into an exam.
- ➢ Plan your future.
- ➢ Enter a new environment.
- ➢ Are interacting with new people.

Positive thinking is universally good. Having it as a habit is success-bringing. Because thoughts and feelings come before actions, positive thinking is even more important. You've learned that and confirmed the Law of Attraction as a universal principle.

But these are only the thoughts and feelings. What are the right habits of action?

Everything that brings you closer to your personal goal is correct. Habits that are directly or indirectly related to your goal are good choices. A bad example would be a weight loss goal where you choose getting up early as a habit. Getting up early is beneficial but is not directly related to diet. So, the good habit of getting up early would in all likelihood not have the desired effect.

Identify suitable micro habits

For now, we are concerned with spotting the appropriate micro habits. "micro habits" is a newly introduced term, appropriate to the subject matter of this book, that refers to specific habits. These habits differ from larger habits in that they are superficially easier to get into and contribute to the larger habits:

Micro habits	Macro Habits
Are special and denote exactly one action.	Are general and describe character as well as other properties.
Contribute to a macro habit.	Are composed of several small habits.
Examples: ➢ Get up early. ➢ Eat more fruit. ➢ Meet more often with friends.	Examples: ➢ Be disciplined. ➢ Healthy living. ➢ Maintain social cohesion.
Require less time to get used to.	Take more time to get used to.
Can be equated with milestones.	Can be equated with a super-ordinate goal.

Small habits, then, are a contribution to the big picture you desire. The macro habit, in its entirety, contributes significantly to the achievement of your goal. Professional success comes to people who are disciplined or skilled – or both. One big habit, that of discipline, for example, requires several smaller habits that, taken as a whole, contribute to the achievement of the goal.

When you look for the micro habits below that are important to your goal, don't have any doubts just because they seem to be small things. Each habit by itself seems insignificant and weak. But in their totality, micro habits bring you closer to your goal.

Task 1

Look at your big goals – not the stage goals (!) – and think about what general character traits and qualities you need to achieve them. The character traits and qualities you write down will lead you to the macro and micro habits. Write down all the macro and micro habits that are possible for your goal. Write down all possible habits first, even if some of them seem unworkable to you. Maybe they will be at a later time. So, write everything down first.

To make it easier for you to carry out the tasks in this lesson, the entire chapter will be laid out using an example. The example is a deficit that you have identified in yourself: You are overweight and generally not living a healthy life. This is problematic in that it shortens your life expectancy in the long run. In the short term, lower well-being and worsened social participation are some consequences. You recognize the problem and want to live healthier. This macro habit of living healthy is your overall goal. This you have paraphrased with adjectives, verbs and other words to make it attractive: Recognition, feel good, pretty, muscular, confident, etc. In order to better achieve the goal and increase motivation, you have also set milestones. These stage goals include integrating exercise into your daily routine and replacing fast-food with vegetables. It is useful to derive micro habits from the stage goals. To integrate exercise into everyday life, the following micro habits are worthwhile, for example:

➤ Go jogging in the evening
➤ Accompany the children to the playground
➤ Take stairs instead of elevator
➤ Prefer bicycle to car
➤ Walk to shopping instead of driving
➤ Get up earlier in the morning and do crunches

This is how micro habits are formed. Of course, other macro habits are also related to healthy living, such as being disciplined. In this sense, you could regularly expose yourself to temptations and resist them to promote your discipline. Thus, numerous macro habits and micro habits come into question for each goal. You are called upon to independently compose your path. In doing so, it will be necessary for you to think around the corner at one point or another in order to find creative solutions. This book cannot take the task off your hands.

Task 2

After you have discovered, and written down, the possible macro and micro habits for you based on your goals and milestones, you select the habits that seem feasible to you at the present time, or that will be in the near future. In this way, you narrow down your choices to what is realistic for you. However, do not cross out the habits that cannot be implemented at the moment, just save them for later.

Continuing with the example, Task 2 would entail, subjecting each of the habits, from the small example list, to an examination for current feasibility:

Habit	Feasibility currently available?	Perspective
Go jogging in the evening.	No.	You always have to take care of your children in the evening. Even on the weekend, this doesn't change.so this habit is not realistic now or in the near future.
Accompany the children to the playground.	Yes.	This is possible. Suddenly you get a flash of inspiration: You can also implement the previous habit through this one. Because if you have to take care of your children in the evening, you can also accompany them to the playground in the evening – especially in summer, when it is still light at 6 or 7 p.m. Maybe jog with your kids to the playground.

Habit	Feasibility currently available?	Perspective
Take stairs instead of elevator.	Yes.	Since you don't suffer from any physical limitations, this habit can be implemented anywhere there are stairs.
Walk to shopping instead of driving.	Yes.	You don't live in a wasteland, you can carry the bags, and you're generally able-bodied, so this habit is also implementable.
Get up earlier in the morning and do crunches.	Yes.	Now you're overcome by your inner critic: You could get up earlier, but you don't trust yourself with this habit because you like to sleep late. One thing is clear: If you have other habits to choose from, you're welcome to postpone this change for a while.

The last habit on the list should tell you that the goal is not to establish habits that overwhelm you "come hell or high water." Proceed in a way that seems feasible for you personally. The lower the demands on motivation and discipline are in the beginning, the easier it is to stick with the change. Over time, the level of difficulty will increase.

Align habits with goals

Speaking of stage goals: Now it's time to match your individual micro habits to your stage goals.

Task 3

Start with the first stage of your big goal and see which micro habits promote the achievement of that stage. Then go to the second stage and add to these micro habits so that the level of difficulty constantly increases.

Applied to the example, a small graphic illustrates roughly in which direction it should go.

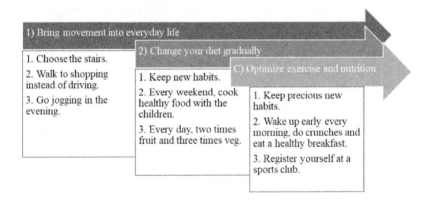

Figure 3: Overarching goal: Healthy living

Gradually building habits brings you several benefits: The added values grow. The challenge behind larger habits is reduced. Synergies between micro habits and the larger macro habits emerge.

If you proceed in the same way as described so far in the first two lessons of this chapter, you will align your habits with your goals. Stage goals and micro habits promote each other, so that they grow together into larger constructs, that promote the onset of a routine, and new larger habits. Do it right! Do it with these strategies!

Lesson 3: Consolidate habits and new structures

The yo-yo effect, the relapse into old behavior patterns – how does this phenomena occur? Something hard-earned does not last. It is replaced again by what we were used to before. At least this is how it happens in some, possibly even in many cases. The frequency of relapses into old habits should not even be debated. Your goal is simply to counteract relapses. The reason for relapse is not that you don't like the new habit or that the added values are not clear. Relapses are due to the simple fact that residuals of the old structures are still present. They are so strongly present that they have the ability to overtake the new habits. Three measures in exactly the order mentioned should be taken to heart in order to reduce the risk of relapse:

1. Be honest with yourself about progress!
2. Allow yourself a generous time frame to complete the transition!
3. Keep the new habits without compromise!

Honesty

Most of the time you notice it yourself when you are being led around by the nose. If at some point you skip a few steps in the retraining process or loosen the leash, you'll notice in your sub-conscious that something is wrong. Don't lie to yourself. Deviations from the planned stage goals have a reason, which is usually to be found in the fact that you do not implement the change as planned. If it happens that you can't keep to something because, for example, you have to visit someone in the hospital or work overtime at work, then there is no question that these are exceptions. However, if there are no valid external arguments and you still deviate from your plan, the reasons for this are to be found within yourself. This is where you need to make adjustments.

Hint!

Exceptions from the targeted goal are not automatically negative. Sometimes exceptions can even have less serious backgrounds (not hospital visits or work related) but be due to a nice evening with friends. If you haven't met in a certain circle of friends for months or years, and only this one evening represents a chance to meet again for the next few years, make the exception! You only live once. Enjoy it. The important thing is that this exception doesn't move you to make more exceptions. You ensure this by letting exceptions really be exceptions; that is, they should happen rarely to very rarely. In addition, Step 1, retraining your thoughts, has helped reprogram your thoughts and feelings so that exceptions are less likely to throw you off balance.

If you notice that you are deviating from the plan, it is useful to take several points of view with the help of the first chapter:

➢ Is there a lack of motivation?
➢ Are the stage goals too far apart?
➢ Are the rewards not enough?

Take these and other questions at hand. Weigh them as objectively as possible. Making minor modifications should help your goals settle back in and keep you from lying to yourself about progress. This will help you recognize when new habits have formed. Once new habits are in place, you will be better able to maintain them by being honest with yourself.

My experience

I never deviated from my positive habits because I was always honest with myself. If I slacked off without a reasonable justification, it was usually due to motivation. For example, when my snacking between lectures increased again and I felt uncomfortable during exercise afterwards, I realized from these clear body-signals that I was on the wrong track. For example, to motivate myself, I decided to reward myself for each week I went without snacking during lectures with a sinfully unhealthy dinner on Sunday. It was always a new dinner to keep things interesting. Another point where motivation was often lacking was when the lectures went worse than I had hoped for with the positive approach. For this case, I had a ritual scheduled for after work: I would pamper myself with a wellness program for the rest of the day once I had mastered the hard day. From then on, whenever the audience made me despair, I almost immediately had a smile on my face. Because I knew: Today, wellness is on the agenda again as a reward!

Patience

You may be longing to have finally acquired the habit you are striving for. Therefore, you might skip certain milestones and proclaim, "I've changed my habit."

The deceptive thing about this approach, is that the euphoria about the supposedly successful change of habit, can hide the fact that you have not yet changed. But as soon as the euphoria has faded away, the previous automatisms tempt you again to follow the old habit. Therefore, always allow yourself enough time, before declaring habits as eliminated and new habits as acquired. For micro habits, you can calculate with the scientific 66 days of adaptation time. For macro habits – depending on age and the strength of the previous habits – several months and up to years are to be expected as a period of adaptation. If it takes years, you will still feel a significant simplification after just a few months. This will be the welcome routine.

Resistance

Both during the adjustment phase and after the adjustment has taken place, it is best if you maintain a certain lack of compromise. If exceptions are appropriate or even necessary, then they are allowed. Otherwise, however, you should concentrate fully on the positive new habits and their retention. The easiest way to ensure consistency is to use specific measures.

> ➤ **Keeping a diary**: By keeping a diary regularly, you can look back on the path you have already taken. This is especially helpful if you've been on the wagon for a while and your motivation is waning, because it will help you to feel proud of a long, successful journey. It would be a shame if you fell off the wagon, wouldn't it? Walked the whole way for nothing? Absolutely not!

- ➤ **Backward visualization**: You've learned to visualize goals before they are achieved, to make them more attractive. Backward visualization highlights existing successes by comparing them to the previous you. You may even have photos of your previous self to strengthen your memory. Backward visualization is authentic because it brings back to light what has already happened, showing you clearly how far you have already come.

- ➤ **Clarify added values**: If you regularly remind yourself of the benefits of what you are doing, it will increase your stamina. All that you've learned so far in this book will help you to achieve this. To enhance backward visualization, we can use the principle of deterrence: If you have recordings, or photos of yourself during your former negative habits, or you can observe other people in the same bad circumstances you used to be in, you can use these things to deter yourself from falling back into old patterns.

Step 3: Methods for acclimatization

To change our habits we need a strategy, and a method. A practical example of how it can work is provided in the documentary, *Macht der Gewohnheit,* by *W wie Wissen,* broadcast on ARD. In addition to expert information, and informative sequences on the subject of habit, the documentary includes an interesting experiment featuring a couple, the Webers, as well as the tattoo artist, Jens. Accompanied by the television crew, the Webers and Jens receive help from psychology professor Wilhelm Hofmann from the University of Cologne, in taking the first steps towards eliminating their negative habits. The fact is it's not easy, because habits are deeply rooted in the brain. Fittingly, Professor Hofmann speaks of a necessary reprogramming.

The first step is to make people aware of the unattractiveness of their habits. They are filmed acting them out (a tool you can also make use of). When you see yourself from the outside for a change, you get a completely different perspective of your situation. The footage of the Webers and Jens reveals the following scenarios:

The Webers are sitting quite far away from each other on the couch. Jennifer Weber is busy with her smartphone, sitting on one corner of the couch, and Bilian Weber is playing with his console in the middle of the couch. This is how they both spend their evening. Both hardly interact. When they see the footage of themselves, their "teeth fall out of their mouths," to use Bilian Weber's words. Jennifer is also not very taken with it: "It's not a nice picture to see yourself like that," she said. Both of them even speak for the first time about it actually threatening their relationship over the long term. Shock at the extent of the negative habit is evident in both of them. In addition, for the first time they do not look at their relationship through rose-colored glasses, but see the danger clearly: relationship breakup, due to lack of interaction. Their ideal is to sit together, talk, and take the occasional evening outing.

Jens passes the time every evening with sweets, potato chips, beer and whisky-cola – not necessarily all in one evening, but at least some of it every evening. In the past, he says, he had his dog as motivation to exercise more. But it has passed away. When he sees himself, his statement is, "Oh, man! When you see it like that from the outside, you think to yourself, somebody ought to step in and stop that." His ideal is to not indulge in his habits on a daily basis, but occasionally he would like to allow them to be his personal kind of indulgence.

The expert, Hofmann is supposed to help. The people are asked to think of strategies to replace the negative habits with positive ones. According to the expert, strong will alone is not enough. As soon as a stressful situation comes, the change of habit wouldn't last if it were built solely on strong will. To make it work we need to substitute the habits with big changes, and stable triggers. Jens quickly comes up with solutions: fruit platters and chewing gum should replace the sweets. The whiskey supplies are too precious for him to give away. Instead, he takes them to the wine cellar. He also gets a new dog. The psychologist is optimistic, because both the replacement habit, and a stable trigger in the form of the dog are in place. The Webers find it more difficult to find solutions. The expert identifies the lack of a positive vision as the cause. Finally, they decide to go out to dinner and watch movies together. At least there are some rapprochements they can make, even if only slightly different from the old habit.

What will happen to the participants after the experiment is still up in the air. According to the psychologist, it's important to get into a rhythm and maintain it consistently. Jens treats himself to another beer after just three days, but otherwise remains consistent. His children enjoy eating with him when he eats fruit and provide him with additional motivation. Jens admits that the habit is not out of his head, the matter is not over for him; that would be too easy. Bilian and Jennifer Weber say they are taking more time off from their smartphones and resolve to see new activities as positive steps forward.

These experiment examples illustrate that positive visions are needed, as well as strategies, because will alone is not enough.

You have already learned these components for successful change.

Chapter 1 highlighted the basic positive attitude needed in thoughts, chapter 2 the motivation, the "attraction", of the change of habits and the will.

Now it's time to look at strategies, the third important component of a transition. This chapter focuses on methods and related tasks, that will help you find and maintain suitable strategies.

Apart from that, interesting insights into science and product creation are given, for you to find useful further assistance in your own transition.

Methods for exercise: weaning and acclimatization

There is no shortage of methods. The trick is to find methods that are universally applicable for retraining. An example of a useful, but less universally applicable method, is anchoring, which is found in Neurolinguistic Programming (NLP).

With anchoring, you choose a gesture, an object, or another similar resource to use, whenever you want to replace the old habit with a new one. In this example, the anchor is a small object that you always carry with you. You take the anchor in your hand, during the practice phase and think of the positive habit you are striving for. The brain is conditioned by this trigger to pursue the positive habit whenever the anchor is touched or held. The more often and consistently you practice, the stronger your brain's programming becomes. If at any time you find yourself in a position where you feel tempted to practice the negative habit, you pick up the anchor, and switch to the positive one instead. If the anchor is strong enough, then with its help, you replace the negative habit with the positive one every time.

The problem with this method of re-conditioning is that it is not applicable to all habits. If you find it difficult to get up early in the morning for example, then this anchor is of no use, because you would have to get up early to condition yourself with the anchor in the first place. If you can't manage to get up early, you can't anchor getting up early either.

Therefore, the following methods are presented as solutions with universal applicability that will show you how to:

- ➤ Put hurdles in the way of negative habits.
- ➤ Reduce barriers to positive habits.
- ➤ Keep the quality of positive habit triggers high.
- ➤ Benefit from other people.

These methods are transferrable to any habit with a degree of creativity.

Lesson 1: Hurdles for bad habits

Hurdles make it harder to pursue an activity. The more hurdles, and the stronger the hurdles are, the less likely you are to pursue the activity. Hurdles are a useful tool for breaking bad habits.

The most practical hurdle is one that makes the habit impossible, or nearly impossible, to practice. If, for example, you tend to consume too much beer or wine in the evening, and are worried that alcoholism could develop from this, then ideally, you'd make it more difficult for yourself to consume alcohol, by not having any at home. This does not make consumption impossible, because the gas station may be nearby. But if you were to buy it at a gas station, there would be further hurdles – like having to go to the gas station, which would mean a lot of effort, and the high gas station price for the bottle of alcohol, which serves as a deterrent. Now creative people might come up with more ideas, like ringing the neighbor's doorbell to ask for a bottle of alcohol or calling a cab driver to drop it off. But this would be either embarrassing or even more expensive. So, the conclusion is: when alcohol is hard to come by in the evening after the store closes, several hurdles arise to pursuing alcohol consumption. The hurdles are high, so not storing alcohol at home is a good measure. Of course, for addicted people, it is quite different from a mere habit, but the principle is the same. Increasing hurdles make the practice of habits more difficult.

My experience

I was helped a lot by the formation of hurdles. It was the first measure I chose on my way to creating positive habits. Right from the start, I knew that getting up early would be the most important thing for me to accomplish. If I could manage it, then I would gain 4 to 5 hours each day. My hurdle was setting 10 alarm clocks and spreading them throughout my apartment. The alarm clocks were time-shifted: First the alarm clock by the bed, so that I really heard it and woke up, a minute later it was the alarm clock a little further away on the closet, then those in the other rooms and so on. After I had switched off all 10 alarms, I was so unnerved that I wouldn't have fallen asleep even if I tried. Over time, I reduced the number of alarms because I was managing to get up by myself at 6 a.m. without an alarm. I gained important and productive hours of life every day with this newly acquired habit.

Ideally, you make sure that hurdles are placed in the way of your bad habits. You can do this by means of a sequence diagram or a mind map, taking your bad habit as a starting point. The following example is of watching TV in the evening. It makes a graphic representation of your choice that illustrates how one hurdle leads to another and gets in the way of your habit:

Figure 4: Mind map bad habit

Task 1

The hurdles in the example are creative; perhaps even too creative. Do with your negative habits as you see fit. Write down every negative habit you find, on a piece of paper, and think about realistic hurdles. For the beginning, these should be small hurdles. If they don't work, feel free to move on to bigger, and more radical hurdles. The fact is that it must be feasible and realistic for you. Afterwards, try out the hurdles to see if they help you with the transition.

Lesson 2: Reducing barriers to good habits

If the erection of barriers makes the practice of habits difficult, or even impossible, the reduction of barriers logically ensures the opposite. The fewer barriers that stand in the way of good habits, the easier they become to practice. The biggest barrier that makes good habits difficult is one's own motivation. Work has been done to overcome this barrier. You made the goal attractive for this purpose and divided it into stages. Besides motivation, however, there are other barriers to practicing good habits that you may not notice.

Lesson 1, which you have just read and will hopefully put into practice with all the means at your disposal, already contributes to a reduction of the barriers to good habits. Thus, it is also a part of the second lesson. In which way? Imagine that you force yourself through various hurdles to get up early in the morning instead of sleeping until 10 or even 12 a.m. Since these hurdles automatically make you achieve your goal of getting up early, the barriers to the good habit are automatically gone.

In simpler terms:

When you set hurdles for bad habits, choose, if possible, hurdles that make the practice of bad habits **impossible.** *This will, at the same time, remove all the barriers that stand in the way of good habits.*

When this approach is not possible, you should think about what specific barriers to positive habits might be standing in your way. Physical barriers are particularly obvious. The more preparations you have to make, or errands you have to run, in order to practice a positive habit, the more detrimental it is. Again, healthy eating serves as an example: What are the possible barriers here?

> ➤ Elaborate recipes: Healthy eating is often associated with elaborate recipes. In fact, a healthy diet can already be covered by high-quality, ready-made food. There is also a large selection of simple recipes available on the Internet. Time estimates, difficulty levels and the scope of the ingredients list, allow conclusions to be drawn about the effort behind a recipe.

> ➤ Availability: If fruits and vegetables are not purchased, they are not available. Thus, the healthy diet becomes impossible. General availability must be distinguished from immediate availability. "Immediate" means that you have the plate of fruit at your fingertips 24/7. "General," on the other hand, can mean that the fruit is hanging on your trees in the plot 50 kilometers away – not very practical. With immediate availability, you're more likely to consume healthy food.

> ➤ Lack of knowledge: Those who are poorly informed, not only do things wrong, but even tend to put mistakes on a pedestal. The tasks are thus judged to be more difficult than they really are. Being broadly informed about a topic actually reduces psychological barriers. Because if you are aware of the simplicity of something, you will develop a greater motivation.

Task 2

Now it's your turn to reduce the barriers to your envisioned new habits. Think about how you can remove mental and physical barriers. "Mental", means acquiring new knowledge, or taking steps to strengthen your motivation. "Physical" provides for actions, using things or objects that entice the practice of the new habit. In the course of these tasks, reconsider your hurdles to the bad habits from Lesson 1. Can these hurdles be transformed, or intensified so that they make the practice of bad habits impossible, and the new habits the only alternative?

The important thing to remember with lessons 1 and 2 overall, is not to overly trust any of the measures. Hurdles to bad habits, for example, may be effective, but setting those hurdles requires a certain amount of self-discipline. People are often gifted at lying to themselves when they need to fight old habits. So, at some point, there may come a time when you'll think you don't need the hurdle anymore. It may be as early as the 3rd or 4th day that you already think, "I'm so sick of having to dig the remote out of the garden bed. I'll stop this nonsense now. For sure, I'm not going to use the remote and the TV anymore." Be sure right now that this is a lie. It's a lie from your inner critic, your second voice, your old habit – your unwanted self. Call it what you will, but no habit is stably eliminated on the 3rd or 4th day.

Did you know?

"Just one more time, just one more time," is often said by drug addicts, alcoholics, and otherwise addicted individuals when they promise to get better. While some individuals compare addictions to habits, science is a bit further along. The difference is that with a habit, the reward signal eventually goes out. Because the person in question has become accustomed to a thing, so a reward is no longer necessary. Drugs, on the other hand, are addictive because they artificially maintain the reward signal through hormonal intervention in processes of the brain. Consequently, you will be spared the extreme struggle, in which every fiber of your being is consumed by just one more time of exercising the habit. But still it is to be assumed that your brain will try to play tricks on you.

So, you must not rely too heavily on your own thoughts, on your way to withdrawal, because they have a high potential for deception. That's why it is important that you plan a firm schedule, during your transition. Up to this point you have the big goal, the important small stages, and the macro and micro habits together. Now it's time to set a fixed schedule for eliminating the negative habits and replacing them with positive habits.

Task 3

Start with your first stage goal, where you determine the time you need, to implement your micro habits: Should the stage goal be achieved within two weeks? Is this realistic? In what order and time frame do you want to set hurdles for each negative habit? In what order and time frame do you want to reduce barriers for the positive habits? When do you set a higher hurdle, if you find that the first hurdle is not enough to defy the negative habit? Define a set of goals, habits, actions, countermeasures, timing, and any other details you can think of.

With respect: Life is not a to-do list. But neither is it a pony farm; especially when it comes to the desire for success, a strict approach is necessary. Of course, some people have an easier time achieving success in their lives. The inequalities are undeniable. That is why some people just have to put in more effort than others. Are you ready to plan accurately and leave nothing to chance? You *will* succeed if you put together a surefire plan. This second lesson, combined with everything you've learned so far, will help you do that.

Lesson 3: Maintain or increase quality of triggers

Positive habits can be initiated by means of triggers. The mere thought of a habit is a trigger. With negative habits that are internalized, the quality of the triggers are high because routines and automatisms have developed. Thoughts of positive habits are a good start, which must be followed by reinforcement of the thoughts. Visualizations and affirmations contribute to reinforcement. So does the reduction of hurdles.

Button up all your triggers and make sure their quality stays high. Increase the quality if necessary. Affirmations have the disadvantage that they are purely mental triggers of positive habits. With visualizations you can do much more. For example, it is possible to regularly add new pictures of yourself, and the path to success, to a pinboard you have made. Before-and-after pictures for physical goals, grades from semesters when studying, pictures of new friends or groups for social goals – these are all possible quality enhancements, for the use of visualizations as triggers. If you reduce barriers to positive habits by acquiring knowledge or picking simple recipes – as was noted in the example – you expand your knowledge base, which is also an increase in the quality of the trigger.

As you can see, it's not just having the triggers that counts, as has been the theme of this book so far. It is important, at least in the long run, to update and optimize the triggers. Not perfection, but progress is necessary.

Lesson 4: Benefit from others

Don't worry it's not about taking advantage of people. This lesson shows you in a moral way how to take advantage of relationships with acquaintances, friends and family to achieve your goals. The greatest benefit you can get is through sharing your goals with other people. Tell as many people as you can about what you plan to accomplish. Even though you may think:

➢ "But that's nobody's business!"
➢ "Ha! And then when i don't make it, everyone laughs their heads off at me. Certainly not with me!"
➢ "I don't know how to do it, though."

On the first point, of course you don't have to share extremely private goals. However, it is good to talk about it, at least with those closest to you. You will thus get your worries and doubts off your chest, which will make you feel better. A few words of encouragement from these people will also help. You don't have to talk to anyone about your complete goal, or the new macro habits you are aiming for. You might as well tell them about micro habits that you want to develop. This way, the overall goal remains secret because you are only telling them about a small fraction of it.

There will be more about the second point on the list shortly. This point has a special place, because in it lies hidden the great secret recipe of lesson 4.

For the 3rd point on the list, it is true that, in conversations with some people, it is difficult to address certain things. There isn't necessarily a natural compulsion to do so. So perhaps, only talk openly with your closest confidants about your plans to develop a successful habit. There are rarely any inhibitions here. Talk to other people about your plans when it arises, for example, because a suitable topic is being discussed.

Task 4

Make a list of people with whom you can easily talk about your plans and intentions, without having to worry about whether your concerns are in the right hands. On another list, write down all the people with whom you have a good relationship. In a third list, write down all the acquaintances you could tell about your plans if the opportunity arises. Even if you think you will never have the courage to talk to some of the people on these lists about your plans, make the lists anyway. After all, no one knows what you will decide to do later...

Now, to the second argument on the list; on which a lot rides:

Telling other people about the plans exposes the risk of being ridiculed by those people once the plans fail.

Advice on the Internet, in books, and from famous personalities, literally overflows with praise for the strategy of first keeping plans to oneself. The pluses for this strategy are plausible. No question about it. Besides the fact that you don't run the risk of being distracted from your goal by negative talk around you, and you don't embarrass yourself in case of failure, you have another advantage – if you succeed, you surprise everyone. When people suddenly see you 30 kilograms slimmer, learn that you have become a millionaire, or hear about your professorship – what a success, they will say!

But think back to what was on the syllabus in chapter 2. You internalized how important positive thinking is. Now, what does it say about your lessons when you hide your plans? Not necessarily something negative, but it certainly can't be said that it's a completely positive basic attitude. Why don't you just assume that other people will speak well of you when they hear about your goals? Do it, tell them about your goals and plans! People will help you. And if not, use the amused comments as a visualization measure. How stupid they will look when you achieve your goal! Visualize your satisfaction to develop even greater motivation.

Besides these facts, the risk of embarrassment if the goal is not achieved is not necessarily negative. After all, motivation and discipline are undoubtedly increased by the fear of embarrassment. In addition, there is the fact that it is basically the same for everyone; we all have dreams, desires and goals. Those who are upfront about their dreams exude *joie de vivre*. They are not afraid of embarrassment; they feel gratitude for life and accept failure easily. In contrast, there are people who talk little about their desires and goals. However, this does not mean that they successfully implement everything they plan. On the outside, these individuals look like doers, but on the inside, they may feel weak. A numerical example provides more clarity: Nicholas formulates 2 goals and achieves both. Cindy formulates 20 goals and achieves

5 of them. To the outside world, Nicholas looks like the doer be-cause he achieves everything. But viewed soberly, the enthusiastic Cindy is the winner in the comparison.

My experience

I am absolutely on fire for talking to other people about the goals I set. In my formation of new habits, I have told many peo-ple about what I plan to do. A few declared me crazy for setting 10 alarm clocks in the morning. Others thought it was creative. The important thing for me in the initial conversations, was to spot the people who were sympathetic to my ideas about changing habits. When I realized that certain people were labeling my in-volvement in the environmental protection association as "brain-cracked" (that was the exact wording) and were almost attacking me personally, I gratefully accepted this, because when a person flares up so negatively, I know I should reduce contact with them. I have learned through conversations with other people, that the objective critics and supporters who can justify their opinions are important. So, I got good insights for the implementation of my change of habits and shared my successes with the supporters. A few people even joined in with some of the remapping, such as my brother, who visited me for 2 weeks and got up with me at 6 a.m. every morning. This motivated me. His laughter at the 10 alarm clocks right in the morning was refreshing for both of us, and heralded the beginning of absolutely outstanding days – pos-itive mornings have a breakthrough effect on the entire day!

The above example is not meant to say that Cindy is better than Nicholas, or that either of them is doing anything wrong. I'm not reinforcing the idea, that it is better to tell everyone about your goals than to keep them to yourself. I'm merely aiming to show, that concerns and fears about other people's reactions, should not be the deciding factor in whether to tell people about your goals. Motivation requires, among other things, enthusiasm, and positive thinking. So, let's bring enthusiasm and positive thinking to the fore! Show both, openly and just *try* to tell other people about your plans in the beginning. No matter how these people react. You provide yourself with additional resources to change by involving other people. Use these resources by seeing the positive in them. You have already learned this. People may even agree to help with the transition, providing additional motivation. Everything is possible – most likely when you act offensively in every respect!

News from the bag of tricks: How science and business make change easier

The impetus to integrate this subchapter into the book was given by the documentary *The Power of Habit,* which has been mentioned several times. In it, researchers from the University of Siegen were presented, who produce small devices to help with negative habits. These devices work by either annoying you, so that the practice of the habit is omitted, or animating you to reflect on whether it is reasonable to pursue the respective habit. Dr. Matthias Laschke and Prof. Marc Hassenzahl, a mathematician and a designer respectively, combined their expertise, and that of their respective teams, to develop the inventions.

The Key Moment – food for thought

Their invention "Key Moment" is designed to make you think. It has a system in which, when you try to grab one of the keys, the other one slips down. The meaning unfolds, precisely when the key associated with the bad habit, is placed on the side where it does not slide down.

To clarify: In the documentary, the classic example of "car vs bicycle" is used. The bicycle should be preferred to the car, as a good habit, in terms of environment, health and exercise. So, the car key is placed in such a way, that when the person tries to grab it, the bike key slips off. Of course, it is up to the person concerned to decide against the bicycle key and take the car key instead. But either way the person cannot avoid thinking about it.

With a little creativity, Key Moment can be used for many other purposes. Imagine you have an allotment for example. The plot gives you company, through the other members of the garden association, as well as exercise and creativity, in the fresh air. On the other hand, there is temptation in one of your rooms at home, namely a PC, where you could "waste" your time, day after day, playing games. You can't manage to give up your bad habit, so you take a key to the room, and you lock it. You attach this key and the key to your plot to Key Moment. Then, whenever you grab the key to the "game room", the key to the plot tumbles down first, and you end up wondering about mowing the lawn today or having a barbecue with other members at the allotment club instead.

You can adapt such Key Moment scenarios with little effort. The scientists from the University of Siegen show that it primarily requires creativity.

Stairs instead of elevator – individual product

An invention that encourages people to take the stairs instead of the elevator has not yet been specifically named and launched. However, it has already been demonstrated. It is a kind of stem that is mounted in, or just outside of the elevator. The stem, when the desired floor is clicked on, talks to the occupant, emitting words recommending they choose the stairs.

The interactive shower curtain – mastering low water consumption

Because the majority of the population in Germany has less to worry about than in other corners of the world with regard to an adequate water supply, there is an increasing tendency for unnecessarily high, water consumption to occur. In some households, water consumption is wastefully high, while in others it is at least higher than it should be. Surprisingly, one's showering and bathing habits are an area where there is less judgment about it than in other areas of life. When, in fact, there are habits in showering and bathing that could also do with being analyzed. People who turn off the water while soaping up in the shower use less water for example. Whereas those who leave the water running continuously, and even shave or brush their teeth in the shower, will tend to waste water.

The scientists at the University of Siegen have also thought about these problems in their interdisciplinary teams. The result is an invention that has been christened the "interactive shower curtain". This shower curtain costs more than a regular one, but it has the bonus of an integrated feature that displays your water consumption, in the form of an animation. Easy to understand, this animation motivates you to use water resources more carefully. In multi-person households it is even conceivable to organize competitions. Different peoples' information can be programmed into the shower curtains' memory and their showering behavior compared with others. Who will soon take the crown as champion of the lowest water consumption?

The power-saving caterpillar – switch off the TV, otherwise it's annoying!

With the power-saving caterpillar, the scientists presented, what is probably the most annoying invention in the documentary. It makes annoying noises if the TV is not turned off completely, or if it is left on for a long time without being watched. It alerts you to turn off the TV after use, so that the power consumption is less than it would be if the TV were left on standby.

Products in free trade

As indicated, you don't have to be a scientist to create products that help kick bad habits.

The "Good Habit Bracelet," which is available to buy at trnd.com, works as a universally applicable aid. Whenever the negative habit is pursued, the bracelet emits light electric shocks. These are not harmful to health, of course, but they are unpleasant. Users can program when the bracelet should emit the shocks. It offers plenty of customization potential, for example, to stop disregarding alarm clocks and get up earlier, or to stop postponing sports activities and follow them immediately. The manufacturer recommends pressing the bracelet itself for non-programmable habits to trigger the electric shock.

In addition to physical products, a range of digital products exist for kicking habits. This doesn't necessarily mean the typical advertised courses from online marketers that cost several hundred euros. Instead, many free, or low-cost apps are available for download from on-line stores. One app –*Streaks* – makes it possible to create up to 12 tasks. Each task corresponds to a negative or positive habit that you want to either eliminate or establish, and success graphs are displayed. Other apps have different approaches. For example, if you follow the method of involving other people in your habit, *Habit Share* proves handy. This application clearly lists your progress to other users. You may be able to find like-minded people through *Habit Share* and gain additional supporters for your transition.

Top 10 unusual habits

In this last chapter, things get more specific, and at the same time, slightly extravagant. Up until now you've been given instructions on how to find meaningful habits that will lead you to success. Here and there you also read examples of popular habits to try out for yourself. But generally speaking, specific advice was used sparingly, because it is highly individualized and doesn't necessarily advance every reader. In this chapter, the top 10 most unusual habits are waiting for you! You will get to know special and partly exotic habits, which do not suit every person, but will definitely be an additional support on your way to success. And I will also share my experiences, with some of the habits that worked for me, and give you tips on how to implement them, to maximize the benefit this last chapter can offer you.

#1 Reduce stress with the same wardrobe

Making decisions is a challenge. You have to weigh between different alternatives, which demands mental resources. For some people, much of this decision-making effort goes into choosing what to wear that day. Especially people who are often in the public eye. After all, they are also under a lot of pressure when it comes to clothing. An amusing example of this is coach Julian Nagelsmann during RB Leipzig's first two games in the 2020/2021 UEFA Champions League. In his first appearance, social media reactions described him as having been dressed like a confirmation boy. While his second appearance earned him comparisons to a senior citizen, with some of the press even questioning him more about his outfit than the game, after the match was over. Perhaps something similar has happened to you with your fashion, being ridiculed by friends or colleagues at work?

Some successful people make it look easy, with former Apple CEO Steve Jobs and current Facebook CEO Mark Zuckerberg being popular examples. Steve Jobs almost always dressed the same, with his trademark classic black sweater. Mark Zuckerberg usually chooses fairly similar clothing and varies only minimally. By having a fixed wardrobe, two main benefits already alluded to occur: First, the amount of choice is reduced – especially in the morning, you want a relaxed and stress-free day, which is where a fixed wardrobe helps. Second, after a few trial runs, a wardrobe crystallizes that does not give rise to any approaches to criticism in public. Thus, fashionable *faux pas* are avoided.

Something that is rarely thought of with a monotonous clothing style, but which nevertheless arises as a potential further advantage, is unmistakability. Over time, it becomes your unique selling point to be spotted in exactly this clothing combination every day. That's how you'll most likely earn yourself a bit of a reputation.

#2 Use cold showers to improve your immune system and mental state

Taking cold showers is a habit that should be familiar from military movies. Often this habit is dismissed as "over-hard" military programming. You would not want to miss the pleasant warm shower or the warm bath after a strenuous day after all! Or would you?

Studies have produced several interesting findings in this regard. In a <u>Dutch study,</u> for example, it was found that, among test subjects, those who took cold showers had 30% less sick leave than those who took warm showers. One plausible medical reason for this is the mobilization of leukocytes by the cold stimulus. Leukocytes are the white blood cells found in blood, tissue, mucous membranes and lymph nodes. They contribute to defense against pathogens and are an essential component of the immune system.

It is possible to strengthen your immune system, and reduce your susceptibility to minor infections, as well as major illnesses by taking cold showers. This gives you more time in full health, which you can use as planned. Infections, on the other hand, will throw a spanner in the works of your plans due to the recovery time.

Furthermore, cold showers can improve your mental state. <u>In a study, scientist Sevchuk</u> determined that cold showers can help with depression or depressed mood patterns. According to the scientist, because of the high density of cold receptors in the skin, it is conceivable that cold showers send multiple electrical impulses from the peripheral nervous system to the brain. This could lead to an anti-depressive effect. His investigation confirmed this assumption, although he admits that further investigations are needed to make scientifically reliable statements.

There must be some truth behind the invigorating power of cold showers for the mind, because there is no other way to explain the many positive experiences that <u>people </u>have in <u>self-tests.</u> Better blood circulation, alertness and increased oxygen intake are among the other benefits highlighted, which is why a cold shower is recommended, especially in the morning before starting the day. Whenever you do it, it's hard to imagine that cold showers won't bring you benefits as a habit!

#3 Drink lukewarm water in the morning as a basis for well-being

Drinking lukewarm water in the morning is an approach that has its roots in the far East, possibly in Japan. How much to drink, sources, and even the Japanese, disagree on. Anything from 1, to 4 glasses seems reasonable. The lukewarm water should be drunk on an empty stomach and before coffee. So, it's the first thing you feed your body after getting up. But why? It is clear that water is essential for survival. But why lukewarm?

First of all, the consumption of water generally sends a digestive impulse to the gastrointestinal tract. But the lukewarm temperature has another effect also: boosting the metabolism. In the morning, when the metabolism is still sluggish, this can be worth its weight in gold. You may be able to digest breakfast better and prevent morning sickness. It is not uncommon for people to complain that they cannot eat in the morning because they get stomach aches. A glass of lukewarm water can solve this problem. Even for people who have had no problems with digestion in the morning so far, there is nothing wrong with starting it already.

There are a number of other benefits that lukewarm water is supposed to give immediately after getting up, they are not proven, although many people do report these improvements. For example, it is said that the intake of lukewarm water in the morning can alleviate complaints or diseases such as high blood pressure, stomach problems, diabetes and constipation. Weight gain can also be prevented, and weight loss in turn can be promoted, because warm water supposedly dissolves the fat components in the digestive tract better.

My experience

I myself am on fire for the glass of lukewarm water. I first learned about the ritual at a project weekend with my team. A colleague, who had spent around 4 years of his life in Asia, had been performing this custom for 10 years. From the very first day, I found it pleasant to drink lukewarm water in the morning. I felt positive effects with my digestion only after several days. All in all, the ritual still works for me today. Another positive side effect, as I see it, is that it encourages an abundant consumption of water. I personally find it easier to reach the recommended 3 liters of water consumption per day in the morning with the lukewarm water, because after about a quarter of an hour I have already drunk more than half a liter.

#4 Eat foods you don't like on a regular basis

An absolutely underestimated habit! It is normal that certain foods do not appeal to you and others even more so. Surely you have noticed that there are people who eat almost everything. Even if they are served something they don't like, they eat it without disgust or grumbling. These people are not even necessarily overweight or not "moderate" in their food habits. They simply have open tastes and a high tolerance level. Those who want to accept things as they are will simply say, "Tastes differ." But those who want to work on themselves and take advantage of a more tolerant sense of taste will say, "Taste can be trained, and so can tolerance."

What advantages does this actually have?

➢ The higher tolerance means that you as a guest no longer have to refuse food that you don't like. In this way, you will presumably make a better impression on your hosts, and you will be spared having to give the unpleasant explanation of why you don't eat something.
➢ You become more open to different foods and test more, which expands your taste horizons. As a result, you can even become a gifted amateur chef.
➢ In emergency situations, where there is less or hardly any food, you are less likely to be picky. Therefore, you are likely to get through the situation better.

This habit is not about giving up your preferences to certain foods. The goal is for you to condition yourself to try all foods, to be open to them, and over time to increase your tolerance to the foods you don't like. There are several ways to do this. One of these ways is the varied preparation or use of foods. For example, there are many people who do not like raw cheese. To them, cheese stinks and nothing will change that. This view is fine. But if you put a pizza topped with cheese on the table for the same people, they wouldn't be so averse. You realize you can approach the taste of your "food dislikes" by processing them differently. For example, you don't have to eat raw ginger right away, but you can use it as a spice and make a warm ginger tea later. In this way, you can slowly feel your way to the taste.

The other way you can change your tastes is the hard way: by planning to eat one or more foods you don't like at certain meals each week. That way, you'll get used to the foods more quickly over time.

My experience

I used to dislike foods like cheese, milk and numerous vegetables. Due to a stay abroad for several months, during which I had hardly any choice in meals due to a strictly timed program, I was regularly forced to eat exactly these foods. Especially the vegetables were always on the program as it was oriental cuisine, and these vegetables could hardly have been more exotic. With the milk I was confronted with goat's milk, which was completely unknown to me – Imagine my doubts! For the first few days with this menu, I was only conditionally enthusiastic. But with time, everything improved. Today I have much more tolerant tastes and even enjoy eating foods that I used to reject! For health, of course, this is also an advantage, because more healthy foods are on the menu.

#5 Let your favorite song wake you up to start the day optimistically

One thing I made use of to help me get up better was multiple alarm clocks at first. When getting up early with a single alarm clock was no longer a problem, I still thought about what I could do to maintain my discipline and get up early while adding a good mood factor. I decided, since I had read it on numerous websites, to use my favorite song as a signal when waking up. Several websites had suggested that my favorite song would help start the day on an optimistic note. So, it was for me as well. I listened and still listen to the song *A real Hero* by the band Electric Youth every morning as a wake-up signal.

Hint: It isn't always your favorite song that is the best choice. An <u>article in the Süddeutsche Zeitung magazine</u> drew my attention to the fact that some songs just don't evoke optimism. In the article, the author reports that during his childhood he used to wake up to Bon Jovi's song *Always*. This schmaltzy rock song may motivate you to get up if it is your favorite song. But at the same time, it has a serious background. This is exactly what the author mentions in the article – people tell him today that he was a serious child.

Accordingly, it would be important for you to choose a song that you like a lot, but at the same time has a positive melody and content. For example, *Happy* by Pharrell Williams would be a selection that could contribute to an optimistic day.

#6 Be proactive early in the day to make it the way you like it to be

This is a habit that Mark Zuckerberg particularly emphasizes in his own case. In his eyes, it is important to be proactive in your daily routine from the beginning of the day.

By this he means:

1. Having concrete ideas of your own about the course of the day ahead.
2. Actively pursuing these ideas right away.

Otherwise, Zuckerberg says, you end up having to spend a large part of the day reacting.

A simple example will help you to understand this: Imagine that you have not planned your day and have no tasks ahead of you, except for perhaps a few obligations. Then someone calls you and asks you for support. You don't want to provide this support because you actually feel like relaxing. But you have no choice because you have no fixed appointments as genuine excuses. Contrast this with a case where you've planned the day exactly and have firmly integrated relaxation into your schedule. You turn off the smartphone and relax in a warm bath or even go for a booked massage. There is no possibility of anyone stopping you from your plans because no one can reach you. In this case, you have proactively designed and implemented your day.

So, plan your day in a binding way so that nothing can get in your way, and eliminate as many disruptive factors as possible for the activity at hand.

#7 Allow the child in you space to feel the joy of being alive

There are some situations when you are overcome with the urge to do something that only children actually do. Maybe it's the leaves lining the streets in the fall that you want to kick away. Maybe you want to balance on the curbs near pedestrian walkways. Or maybe you just feel like acting completely silly and making weird faces in public. Basically, there is nothing wrong with giving in to all of these temptations because they are not negative impulses. For example, you wouldn't want to make weird faces if you were sad or worried. Balancing on curbs near pedestrian walkways can be a sign of lightness and a desire to be active.

Since you are not a child, you should be careful with some things. This is the case with grimaces, for example, as other people might feel offended. But as long as you do it thoughtfully, the appeal is there for you to get into the habit of leaving plenty of room for the child in you. Even build regular phases into your daily or weekly routine, where you pursue childlike activities for 15 minutes. Try out what suits you — often it can even be difficult just to categorize something as strictly childlike, let alone do it.

Warren Buffet, the US multi-billionaire, has developed a childlike eating habit. If you believe his statements, he eats ice cream and drinks cola every day. His reasoning: he has found that children have the lowest mortality rates. Since they prefer to eat ice cream and cola, he has incorporated these foods into his diet. How much truth there is behind this abstruse comparison remains to be seen. In any case, he is now 90 years old and healthy.

It is best to choose kid-friendly activities that are beneficial to your health though and that increase your activity levels at the same time. Then you will benefit in more ways than just one. It's quite possible that after you have been childlike a few times, you will develop a greater zest for activity and life, as well as looseness.

#8 Double check everything to bring security into your life

The line between ensuring security, and the less desirable need for control can be fine. Therefore, you should not overdo it with this habit and only double-check everything, while not excessively checking 5 or 10 times. According to relatives, rap icon Eminem from the USA only goes to sleep once he has personally double-checked all windows and doors. If they are closed, then he can fall asleep in peace and safety. This is not unreasonable, because 1) what's wrong with a little check, during which you might notice other important things, and 2) hasn't it happened to you that you forgot to close a door or a window? This is not only about burglary protection, but also about well-being. After all, if you come into your office room in the morning during winter after the window has been open all night, then your motivation to work will quickly vanish.

Checking that the stove is off before you go out saves potential hazards. Making sure that everything that doesn't need to be on is really turned off before you leave work, saves electricity and possibly less hassle with your boss too. Double-checking makes sense in many ways, including the supplies in the fridge; Is there really enough milk left, or am I confusing the current situation with a picture from last week that I still have in my head? Double check everything, but not unnecessarily often. Also important is to check first and foremost what you are responsible for. Just don't start messing with other people's business without good reason. Otherwise, you will quickly lose sympathy or gain a reputation as a control freak.

#9 Play through important conversations and situations in your head to be prepared for anything

This is an unconscious habit that many people have. They imagine an event that is yet to come, and go over the associated conversations, and processes in their head. Sometimes they imagine themselves succeeding. This is a helpful visualization method. Pessimists do it the other way around and sometimes upset themselves by imagining someone telling them off in conversation, or otherwise imagining bad processes.

Make this a controlled conscious habit that you use as preparation for important conversations and moments in your life. By imagining the various progressions, objections, challenges, and more, you can at the same time better influence the flow of the conversation in reality. As life repeats certain patterns in conversations, you will benefit from being prepared for more situations in your life through regularly practicing this.

My experience

For a while, I wasn't necessarily imaginative when talking to women and I couldn't handle small provocative remarks well. These and other difficulties made dating conceivably difficult for me. At some point, I started imagining dates and different conversation processes. In the process, I came up with various counters, compliments, anecdotes, and similar ideas. At some point, I started dating women again and prepared specifically for them: name origin, nationality, or culture, and much more. The goal was never to manipulate people, but to be able to contribute more to conversations. After some time, I realized that my training, which was geared towards dating, helped me in all kinds of conversations – even professional ones! I had, and still have, almost always the right words ready to act and react.

#10 Walk barefoot more often for greater well-being

Steve Jobs liked to do it in the office: Barefoot running. In fact, if you look at people in parks, schools, universities, gyms and numerous other places in recent years, a small trend has developed around this practice. Opponents say it's unsanitary. So, the advice is that you don't walk barefoot in restrooms and other spaces where high numbers of germs are likely to be. But there is almost nothing against walking barefoot on grassy areas, even on pedestrian walkways and, if it is allowed, in offices. In fact, there may be several advantages.

Feet consist of numerous small muscles, tendons and receptors. A shoe that promotes the foot's natural posture when walking is rare, which often leads to a regression in foot health in the long run. Barefoot walking prevents this. The likelihood of foot and nail fungus can be reduced, and better mobility, as well as a greater sense of well-being – especially in the warm months – can be enhanced.

Closing words

"But it's a habit, you can't get rid of it that easily." As you've probably already noticed, this phrase, which is often used as an excuse, is completely true. There are 2 main approaches to you remain consistently on the ball. One is to keep problems and difficulties a secret. The other approach is to be open about what the challenges are. The latter is probably the better approach. It might be difficult to remain motivated in the face of the many challenges that lie ahead. But having walked the walk, you are much more crisis resistant and capable of dealing with problems as they arise. Hopefully, the openness of this guidebook will encourage you to be just as open with yourself.

You have learned how deceptive the human brain can be. Don't fool yourself into thinking that everything is going to be easier than this guidebook says. This is the last, and perhaps most important lesson you can learn. Go carefully through every detail, and every step of the transition – including the pitfalls. And prepare yourself for the possible obstacles. Take all the hints and tasks seriously because your success depends on it. Don't feel too tired, or too silly to perform the tasks that challenge you. Through practice, you can ensure the achievement of plans, antidotes to problems, and ultimately, a sustainable transition.

Readjustment is not an easy undertaking. In addiction therapy and in other therapeutic branches, it is often recommended not to set long-term goals. This has been covered in the section on stage goals but get into the habit of thinking in even smaller stages every day. You don't have to avoid a habit for several months at first, but only for the next day. At best, you can develop this thought anew every day. Because although you are only talking about the next day, the regularity of this sentence covers a long time period in the end. You have the chance, through these types of thought processes, to use the self-deception mechanisms of the brain, to your advantage. Only creativity stands between you and further resources for success.

Creativity is a source of success anyway; the more creatively you think, the more options you will find, to put up barriers to bad habits, and reduce those to good habits. The more creatively you think, the more ways you will find to make your visualizations appealing. The more creatively you think, the better you will be, at using adjectives to describe your goals, and the more motivation you will develop. Therefore, use techniques such as mind-mapping or tabular representations where recommended. Enrich the recommendations of this book with further creative techniques. In this way —and only in this way — you will be able to exploit it to its full potential.

Meanwhile, never underestimate the effectiveness of a measure. This applies to the positive as well as the negative. You have registered how effective micro habits are. Never doubt that an action will have some effect. Nothing positive is too little to not to be effective. Likewise, nothing negative is too little to be a risk. All the more important, is adherence to the clear plans and structures that you have been given, and have developed for yourself, also. Do not, under any circumstances, allow relapses to occur in your transition. If you feel the tendency to relapse, you should always loosen the leash first by establishing the positive habits at a slower pace. "Better to take an extra month to get accustomed, than to break down after a long road because you overestimated yourself," should be your motto. And in reference to the opening words of the entire book – humans are not machines, of course! You have your own strengths and weaknesses at a core level. Negative habits are the expression of those weaknesses. Denying them, or not taking them seriously enough, and going too fast in the process of retraining, would automatically backfire.

Openness towards yourself, consistency in following the advice in this book, creativity and appreciation towards any success or danger, no matter how small – these are the last words that should remain in your mind. Everything else is a matter of practice. New habits are a matter of practice. Practice makes you a master. Become the master of your success and not of your failure!

And what if it does turn out to be failure? Then remember that every failure can be followed by a success that outshines everything that has gone before. Great movers and shakers on the world stage, VIPs, and talents, have become successful only after several failures. But they never stopped believing in success. If things don't work out, feel free to put the book aside for a few weeks or months to think about potential improvements. Then start your way again, because that's the main principle: keep going, keep going! Isn't that the best habit of all you can develop?

References and further reading

Literature:

A. Florack, M. Scarabis, E. Primosch: Psychologie der Markenführung. München: Verlag Franz Vahlen, 2007.

Byrne, R.: *The Secret – Das Geheimnis*. München: Random House GmbH, 2007.

Clear, J.: *Die 1%-Methode – Minimale Veränderung, maximale Wirkung*. München: Wilhelm Goldmann Verlag, 2020.

Cabane, O. Fox: *Das Charisma-Geheimnis – Wie jeder die Kunst erlernen kann, andere Menschen in seinen Bann zu ziehen*. München: Münchner Verlagsgruppe GmbH, 2020. 3. Auflage.

Ganseforth, H.: *NLP - Neurolinguistisches Programmieren. Wissenschaft, Magie oder Methode?* Studienarbeit: 2004.

Eker, T. Harv: So denken Millionäre – Die Beziehung zwischen Ihrem Kopf und Ihrem Kontostand. Kulmbach: Börsenmedien AG, 2006. 6. Auflage.

Ready, Romilla; Burton, Kate: *Neuro-Linguistisches Programmieren für Dummies*. 2. Nachdruck, Wiley-VCH Verlag GmbH & Co. KGaA (2014)

Online:

http://paedpsych.jku.at/cicero/LERNEN/AllgemeinesLernmod
ell.pdf

https://www.marathonfitness.de/gute-gewohnheiten/

https://onlinelibrary.wiley.com/doi/abs/10.1002/ejsp.674

https://www.deutschlandfunk.de/denken-fuehlen-handeln-wie-
das-gehirn-unser-
verhalten.700.de.html?dram:article_id=80426

https://medlexi.de/Gro%C3%9Fhirnrinde

https://www.pharmazeutische-zeitung.de/ausgabe-
462017/placebo-effekt-wirkung-ohne-wirkstoff/

https://www.spektrum.de/lexikon/biologie/unterbewusstsein/
68591

https://www.geo.de/wissen/gesundheit/22098-rtkl-
psychologie-es-gibt-keinen-hinweis-dass-ein-
unterbewusstsein-existiert

https://www.youtube.com/watch?v=lVhFhR_lSdw&feature=yo
utu.be

https://siga-
fsia.ch/files/Ausbildung/Abschlussarbeiten/XUND_Lu
zern/2018_Diplomarbeit_Andrea_Birchler.pdf

https://www.wissenschaft.de/umwelt-natur/was-das-gehirn-
empfaenglich-fuer-ratschlaege-macht/

https://www.psychologie.uzh.ch/de/bereiche/dev/lifespan/erle
ben/berichte/mehr-berichte-1/selbstwertgefuehl.html

http://www.report-psychologie.de/nc/news/artikel/der-
einfluss-emotionaler-bilder-auf-das-gehirn-2011-12-22/

https://www.wiwo.de/erfolg/management/coaching-und-
motivation-marketing-oder-methode-der-streit-ueber-
die-neurologische-fernsteuerung/24674220.html

https://wordassociations.net/de/

https://www.zeit.de/zeit-wissen/2013/02/Psychologie-
Gewohnheiten/seite-4

Stangl, W. (2020). Stichwort: „Motivation". Online Lexikon für
Psychologie und Pädagogik.

WWW: https://lexikon.stangl.eu/337/motivation/

Stangl, W. (2020). Stichwort: „Disziplin". Online Lexikon für
Psychologie und Pädagogik.

WWW: https://lexikon.stangl.eu/5158/disziplin/

https://www.spektrum.de/news/sucht-und-gewohnheit-im-
gehirn/1399787

https://www.trnd.com/de/toptrnd/ein-armband-gegen-
schlechte-gewohnheiten

https://futurezone.at/apps/5-apps-mit-denen-man-schlechte-
gewohnheiten-los-wird/400945208

https://www.aerztezeitung.de/Medizin/Wer-sechs-bis-acht-
     Stunden-pro-Nacht-schlaeft-lebt-am-laengsten-
     232317.html

https://www.rki.de/DE/Content/Gesundheitsmonitoring/Stud
     ien/Adipositas_Monitoring/Verhalten/PDF_Themenbl
     att_Schlaf.pdf?__blob=publicationFile

https://www.medicalnewstoday.com/articles/323145

https://www.aerzteblatt.de/nachrichten/105181/Soziale-
     Kontakte-im-mittleren-und-spaeten-Lebensalter-
     koennten-Demenzrisiko-senken

https://www.focus.de/gesundheit/gesundleben/fitness/studie-
     zeigt-wer-soziale-kontakte-pflegt-lebt-
     gesuender_id_10851369.html

https://www.tagesspiegel.de/wissen/studie-ueber-einsamkeit-
     soziale-kontakte-verlaengern-das-leben/1892120.html

Printed in Great Britain
by Amazon

18099606R00078